OLD HOUSES
of New England

THE MACMILLAN COMPANY
NEW YORK · BOSTON · CHICAGO · DALLAS
ATLANTA · SAN FRANCISCO

MACMILLAN & CO., Limited
LONDON · BOMBAY · CALCUTTA
MELBOURNE

THE MACMILLAN CO. OF CANADA, Ltd.
TORONTO

The Fairbanks House. Dedham, Mass.

OLD HOUSES
~ of ~
NEW ENGLAND

BY KNOWLTON MIXER

Photographs by the author except as otherwise noted

New York
THE MACMILLAN COMPANY
1927

Acknowledgments

THIS volume is not the work of an architect nor that of an historian but aims to present typical old houses of New England as an expression of its unique history and as illustrating the liberation of thought which took place through the succeeding generations which built them.

Authority has been sought for the historical background in the standard works on New England such as those of Palfrey and John Fiske, State histories and historical sketches of special phases as well as in books of critical comment, such as "The Causes of the War of Independence," by Claude Van Tyne.

Original sources when available have also been consulted, including Winthrop's Journal, "The Wonder Working Providence of Zion's Saviour," by Captain Edward Johnson, "The Cobbler of Agawam," the "Letters of Roger Williams," "The Journal of Sarah Kemble Knight," Washington's Diary, etc. Most of all is the writer indebted to the local historians of New England for actual data concerning the houses and their builders. Too much praise cannot be given to those devoted New Englanders who in the various towns have with infinite labor and patience accumulated the facts of their localities and recorded them for the enlightenment of those who follow. Theirs has been a labor of love and often the work of a lifetime. Such local histories, for example, as those of George Sheldon of Deerfield, and Thomas Waters of Ipswich, portray the simple or the tragic annals of the generations which are past in most readable and entertaining guise, as do the "Old Dartmouth and Nantucket Sketches," of Henry Barnard Worth and the delightful "Rambles About Portsmouth" of George Ellis. Such contributions make study a recreation and investigation a pleasure.

In the field of architecture the intent has been to trespass as little as possible. First and foremost, the very valuable works of Isham and Browne, in their "Early Rhode Island Houses" and "Early Connecticut Houses," make one wish that they had extended their labors further so as to include all of New England. As covering the entire field, the authoritative volume of Fiske Kimball on the "Domestic Architecture of the American Colonies and of the Early Republic" furnishes a valuable background for the student or amateur.

Local architectural studies such as the "Colonial Architecture of Salem," by Cousens and Riley, "Portsmouth Architecture," by R. Clipston Sturgis, and the "Early Domestic Architecture of Connecticut," by F. Fred Kelley apply the technical test admirably to specific houses. The "Old Houses of Connecticut," published by the Connecticut Society of the Colonial Dames of America, edited by Bertha Chadwick Trowbridge, is a contribution of great value to the subject but of such elaboration and cost that it is available only for reference through the larger libraries.

The writer is grateful for the use of the files of *Old Time New England*, the magazine of the Society for the Preservation of New England Antiquities, and other valuable data from that Society through its corresponding Secretary, Mr. Appleton, and, finally, to the many households into whose interiors he has been permitted to venture and to whose family records he has been made hospitably welcome, he owes a great debt of gratitude. This part of his labor has been both a pleasure and an inspiration.

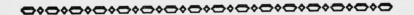

Introduction

OUR PURITAN HERITAGE

◊○◊○◊○◊ HE old houses of New England manifest their origin in the shires of Old England from which T their builders came; they express also in their many additions the progressive life of the succeeding generations. In their individual types they indicate the original status of the owner and something of the purpose which he brought with him, while in the variation of their development they express both change of ownership and variation of idea following the progress of the thought of the community.

The roots of these primitive homes reach back into the English Middle Ages and in themselves represent a persistence of the idea of individuality, in contrast to the growing power of monarchy, which accompanied the Renaissance on the continent of Europe. It was in protest against the attempt of the Stuarts to absorb into the ruling power the right of the individual to do or to think as he pleased, more definitely the latter, that moved many rectors of the Church of England to abandon livings held under the Crown and with their flocks to shake the dust of their native villages from their feet and to go into voluntary exile. This exile led them first to Holland, whose toleration towards all shades of religious belief made her a haven of refuge for the oppressed, and later to the shores of the New World where their purpose was to establish, not a community whose criterion should be a complete freedom of religious thought, but a church-state modeled on their own conception of the Mosaic law. Fleeing a state of intolerance at home, they proceeded, mortal wise, to establish a state of intolerance abroad, under which they undertook to bar, through the ungentle pressure of the stocks, the lash and even the gallows, those who persisted in differing with their conception of man's proper relation to his God. This was necessary if they were to maintain their idea of a church-state.

It was fortunate for our future as a people that this rigidity of doctrine was accompanied by a well-developed idea of civil and political liberty and of the inherent right of the individual to the expression of his own ideas. It is fortunate also that the Puritan revolt drew to this promised land a high quality of citizenship selected from the best of the gentry and yeomanry of old England. The unsuccessful attempt to implant absolutism on the free-born Englishman resulted in England's losing a small but very important section of its best, the very bone and sinew, so far as it went, of the nation, just as the revocation of the Edict of Nantes permanently removed from France a large and important element of the most enlightened of her people, which in some degree also went to the upbuilding of the new nation across the sea.

The concept of civil liberty, therefore, in the long run modified the rigidity and the self-righteousness of the revolting parsons and the complete separation of church and state in New England was finally achieved through the bloodless revolution which seated the Prince of Orange on the throne of England, re-established Parliamentary rule and confirmed the freedom of religious worship.

The acceptance of the idea of the religious as well as the political rights of the individual was, however, not attained in New England without several generations of struggle. The early chronicles of practically every section of the growing communities are marked by the recurring religious differences in which the rigid minority is less and less able to enforce its rule on the revolting majority.

Our ancestors were apt at controversial argument and as their ideas were largely centered on the religious theme, the expounding of doctrine was a function often assumed by even the humblest member of a congregation. A most healthful discussion was therefore constantly in progress. The method adopted to settle an argument in the early days was the forcible ejection from their midst of the minority, and the exodus of the latter toward the frontier where, in spite of hardship and the rigors of climate and attacks of the Indians, they managed to establish communities which grew and prospered sufficiently finally to leaven the whole lump with the leaven of religious liberty. The expanding of the colonies and the founding of separate communities was, as it turned out, hastened by these religious differences.

The major part of the Puritan emigration to America was about coincident with the Long Parliament in England. As the Puritan party led by Cromwell then became dominant at home the exodus to America ceased and the colonies in New England, remote from the homeland and now practically left to themselves, proceeded to develop from within. This development proceeded apace, the colonists, filled with that genius for self-government which generations of struggle with the Crown had given them, organized each community as a self-governing body deriving its powers from the votes of the majority of eligible voters. Eligibility was entirely a question of religious belief and was restricted in the dominant communities to those who were acceptable as communicants in the Church. A fellow of Oxford or Cambridge, even a Baronet's son might sit on the Board of Selectmen of his town with a craftsman or a miller but no Episcopalian was admitted, even to citizenship, in the beginning. The towns scrutinized with great caution the qualification of new applicants and, particularly on the religious side, shades of doctrine were deemed of great importance. Grants of land and rights to the Cow Commons were made to those who were accepted, and once admitted, the community assumed responsibility for their welfare and exacted in full measure, their contribution to the common needs.

Organization extended from the localities to the colonies and in 1643 the Confederacy arose of "The United Colonies of New England" and each colony sent delegates to the General Court. This body represented the interest of all the colonies in their struggle with the home government and was effective in organizing their defense in the devastating war of King Philip.

The Confederacy included at first Plymouth, Massachusetts Bay, New Haven and Connecticut, thirty-nine towns with a population of about 24,000. Maine at this time had a proprietary charter in control of Sir Ferdinando Gorges. New Hampshire had been settled by the followers of Mason and Gorges and by those of Mrs. Hutchinson and was, therefore, both Episcopalian and heretic. Rhode Island, which had united with the colonies of Aquidneck, purchased by

Mrs. Hutchinson, and that of Roger Williams at Providence, was established on the principle of full religious toleration and was the avowed haven of every shade of religious belief. In 1644 and 1648 she applied for admission to the Confederacy but was refused as not possessing a sufficiently stable government.

Of the four colonies composing the Confederacy, Plymouth was less rigid and more tolerant than either Massachusetts Bay or New Haven, in which the theocratic idea ruled. Connecticut, on the other hand, was much more liberal than New Haven.

This Confederacy was the first American experiment in federation and the union, of itself, tended to break down rigidity, yet the separate colonies by their own acts had kept, up to this time, the communities exclusively Puritan and they so remained for three quarters of a century. The movement was essentially ethical and as such could at any time change its form and did so through a gradual process following the break-up of the church-state idea.

After the Puritan exodus from England and during the following century but three minor emigrations were added which differed in doctrine or race, amounting to perhaps five hundred families all together. In spite of these infusions, at the end of the XVIIIth century, New England remained purely English in taste and inclination, populated as it was with the descendants of country squires and yeomen of old England.

This population of 26,000 in 1640 continued to multiply by itself with but little change until the beginning of the XIXth century. After the Revolution, the migration of New England families westward began to spread from New

York to California. Their passage across the continent has been marked by the transplanting of the principles of self-government which have marked their growth in New England. And their progress has been registered by the names of the New England towns from which they came.

The descendants of the Puritan families have thus spread all over our country and have intermarried with other elements in the communities into which they have moved. John Fiske in his "Beginnings of New England," published in 1889, estimated that these descendants were responsible for at least a quarter of the population of that day, that is, about fifteen million persons. Even though the proportion may now have somewhat varied, there can be no question but that this inheritance still constitutes a large and very important element in the life of our day.

Many of the dwellings, even a number of those built in the XVIIth century, remain as monuments to mark this unique development of a peculiar people. They have now become the shrines to which each summer from every state in the union their descendants make their annual pilgrimage. The family, in many cases now grown to an army of thousands, has united its members to preserve the ancient dwelling. Many remain to be so conserved, still occupied by the last direct descendant, a single gentleman who has outlived his near relations or two or three maiden ladies, the last of their family; for the families which have remained behind have intermarried with each other and have gradually dwindled, as is the way of those who have withdrawn from the main stream of life. The charm of their remoteness and that of their ancient houses is the greater for its contrast with the intense activity of our commercial progress.

Taken as a whole, the development of the New England homestead, expressing the life of its period, constitutes an American style which, as already mentioned, has its roots far back in mediaeval England and in its progress has borrowed much from Jacobean and Georgian England, yet the product, adapted to conditions and to materials of the new world, differs characteristically from its prototypes.

This development, while fairly homogeneous, offers variations due to differences of religious thought, of occupation and environment, traced in the foregoing, and these variations have formed the basis of our selections. The first two chapters expound the theme of which the later chapters are the elaborations.

Contents

OLD HOUSES
of New England

OLD HOUSES
of New England

CHAPTER I

DEVELOPMENT OF THE NEW ENGLAND HOMESTEAD

THE PRIMITIVES

THE dwellings thrown together by the devoted band who faced the rigor of the first winter at Plymouth were undoubtedly of the kind chosen as the refuge of man under similar conditions in all ages. The walls were built stockade-like, with saplings fresh hewn from the forest driven into the ground at right angles to a hillside, the latter sufficiently excavated to form the rear of the enclosure and facing the south, that whatever warming ray of sun might penetrate the almost continuous pall of cloud, could be drawn in to supplement the efforts of the pioneers to preserve existence. Rude openings were left in the front and protection from the weather assured by such thatch as was available. This makeshift was soon superseded by a slightly more permanent structure. De Rassieres, who was sent by the Dutch of New Netherland as envoy to Plymouth in 1627, by which year the colony was permanently established, describes the houses as built of "hewn planks." Certain other things are known of these early dwellings as, for instance, that the chimneys were constructed of wood "catted" and daubed

I

with clay and that sea grass was used as thatch in the fashion of English cottages.

Of these earliest cottages none remain. Within fifty years of the first landing they had been replaced throughout the colony by more permanent structures and the homes of the colonists had begun to assume a characteristic style.

The first permanent house followed the outline of the English village cottage but varied in its adaptation to the different settlements. The style adopted by Roger Williams' colony of Providence differed distinctly, not only from Massachusetts and Connecticut, but also from that of Newport and the South County of Rhode Island which partook of the Connecticut fashion. The first two illustrations deal with the primitive house of this Providence type.

Rectangular, nearly square, the large chimney of stone built in and supported by the end wall was its most important feature. One story in height with a steep roof readily to shed water, the peak provided an attic with a small window at the end opposite to the chimney. Entrance to the attic was by ladder at the side of the chimney or by a narrow stair against the rear wall. It was used not only for the storage of supplies but as a convenient harbor in which to stow the children for the night. The ground floor was of earth. The sills and the framing of the house were generally of oak, occasionally of pine, hewn with the adze from a tree as nearly as possible of the size required. As it was much easier to leave the log merely squared, within the limits of its circumference, than to cut its dimensions, the framing timbers were generally much larger than was required. Such beams of oak still exist eighteen inches by eighteen inches. The attic floor was supported by a transverse beam, sometimes two, called the "summer." The origin of the term is given as "sumpter" since it carried the burden of the floor above. These timbers generally ran at right angles to the chimney, resting on the heavy oak plate of the frame and the chimney girth which were in turn supported by heavy posts at the corners. These posts as well as the summers are visible in all old houses where they have not been deliberately covered up.

But few of the early houses had studs, and the weight of the upper story and roof was generally carried on the heavy posts. The sills, equally heavy, usually rested on a thin foundation of stones laid in clay or entirely without mortar. That this simple method of construction was substantial and practical is shown by the existence of many of these frame buildings after two hundred and fifty years, the rotting of the oak sills in contact with the earth being often the only sign of weakness in the old structures.

The chimney and end wall were built of stone laid up with clay and straw, no lime being available for mortar in the earliest period in most sections. The roof was probably originally thatched. For this thatch was substituted at an early date the hand-rived shingle. In some localities, such as eastern Long Island and Nantucket, the shingles were used for sheathing the outside walls of the houses as well as the roof. In northern Massachusetts and other localities the narrow clapboard is used, nailed with hand-wrought nails. The term was originally "clay-board" since it was used to cover the clay and rubble with which the wall was filled. This filling was not only for warmth but also for protection against the arrow of the ever-present enemy. The walls, in many cases, were of the English half timber construction in the first place and the "clay-board" was added later merely as a covering. A layer of stones and clay was sometimes laid under the ground floor when there was no cellar to keep out the moisture. The timbers were tenoned and mortised into each other and held by wooden pegs until the advent of the modern bolt and nut.

Enough has been said to indicate that building among our forefathers was the work, not of carpenters and masons who threw together machine-made material under the supervision of a foreman and an architect, but that of craftsmen who sought and produced their own raw material and wrought with the tools brought from England which their ancestors had used since time beyond memory.

The houses were generally "raised" with the help of the neighbors, as was the case in more recent times in barn raising. The craftsman prepared his framework on the ground and when the parts were ready to be joined together the countryside was called in and with many hands the frame was knit together in short order. This was a time of great rejoicing. The addition of a new house meant a strengthening of the community, added hands to hold a gun or to drive a plough as the need might be, and incidentally added free men to man the breach against the encroachments of autocracy. It was a time of eating and drinking after the framework had been raised, and even the discipline of the stocks was not sufficient to prevent the relaxing of the rigor of daily conduct and the indulgence beyond Puritan limits.

With every emigration came craftsmen. It was an important part of the Puritan plan that they should be included, and in the later emigrations, such as that of New Haven and of Portsmouth, skilled craftsmen were brought directly from England to build for the minister, a man of property, in the one case, and for the rich merchant in the other, more substantial and elaborate dwellings whose plan and construction followed those of the English manor houses.

Occasionally the early houses were built entirely of stone laid with clay and straw. This followed more exactly the

The Waite-Potter House. Westport, Mass.

English model, but the material at hand, more easily handled and worked, was wood and it was therefore generally employed. But few stone houses which can be credited to the XVIIth century remain, and as typical of the more common wooden structure of the earliest period the Waite-Potter house at Westport, New Bedford, is shown. This is the nearest approximation available to the cottage, presumably built between the landing and 1640 or 1650 in the Providence fashion. Though actually built in New Bedford fifty years later it seems to fit recorded descriptions of the earlier dwellings in that district.

The older part of this cottage, shown at the right of the photograph, was built by Thomas Waite about 1677 and remained in this family until 1728. The original stone end of the old house can be seen above the roof of the later ell supporting, the stone chimney. This chimney provides a fireplace whose opening is nearly as wide as the house and faces the single room eighteen feet square. The low attic is reached by narrow stairs along the wall opposite the entrance door. Originally there was no floor. The brick chimney leaning up against its stone ancestor was added to provide a fireplace in the ell which was built at the time of the Revolution. The chimney jamb in the old part is eighteen inches square. The chimney itself is laid up in mortar in which the element of lime is provided by crushed sea shells. This house was originally and always has been a farmer's cottage and has no special significance except its age and typical construction. The roofs of both sections have of course been renewed as well as the front wall shingles.

The Puritan stock multiplied rapidly. Large families were the order of the day and it was not long before the primitive single-room cottage overflowed and the need of additional space became imperative. Expansion could be had vertically or horizontally. It naturally followed the tradition which was, in this case, the end chimney, and the house, retaining this feature, expanded upward. The evolution of the Waite-Potter house is therefore the James Greene house, of Buttonwoods, just south of Providence, Rhode

Island. Here we have an end-chimney, oblong house, two stories and an attic. In the photograph the brick wall may still be seen projecting above the ell in the foreground. The fireplace on the first floor has a twelve-foot opening, the summer and posts are exposed in the "Hall" or living room,

The James Greene House. Buttonwoods, R. I.

and the original windows remain in the east end, not shown in the photograph.

This house was built by James Greene of the third generation. John Greene came to Providence with Roger Williams in 1640. His sons were John, Thomas, James and Peter. The builder was the son of James and the grandson of John. The date, while not known, was probably before 1700.

These houses are seldom seen in their original form and the imagination must be used in most cases to visualize the primitive lines of the building. To this house has been added two lean-tos, the rear lean-to was added first, as is usually the case, leaving the house two stories in front and one in the rear, the rear lean-to providing here, as elsewhere, the kitchen. The west lean-to in the foreground was added a generation later. The houses which have stood the test of time exhibit in their many additions the growing needs and the expanding fortune of the family. Often the parents, rather than build a new house, added an ell for the young people and although after generations of ells the primitive characteristics may be lost, the charm of the old house which rambles north, south, east and west, is enhanced.

In Massachusetts the expansion to meet growing needs was generally lateral rather than upward. Many of the Massachusetts houses, however, started as the one room cottage with end chimney, although the chimney was not made part of the wall in most cases as in Rhode Island. In Connecticut likewise the typical early house consists of two rooms with chimney between and stairway in front of the chimney. The entry in Connecticut is, as a rule, somewhat deeper than that of Massachusetts but this and other differences are of detail only.

The Jethro Coffin house of Nantucket is fairly typical of both colonies. The shape and location of the chimney as well as the prevailing custom of the period indicate that the house was in all probability built originally as it stands to-day, a one and a half story central chimney dwelling including the lean-to. In this old house we have the short, steep front roof and long rear sweep so characteristic of the old Nantucket houses. It was built but little later than the Waite-Potter house, that is in 1686, but is plainly a more developed and substantial dwelling. It is the oldest house standing on the island.

Tristram Coffin, the first of all the Coffins, settled in the town now known as Haverhill, Massachusetts, in 1642.

The Jethro Coffin House. Nantucket.

From there he moved to Newbury where we will hear from him again as establishing that branch of this prolific family about 1650. To Nantucket he moved about ten years later and made the last his final resting place.

His oldest son Peter married Abigail Starbuck, daughter of Edward Starbuck of Nantucket, origin of all the

Starbucks of whose family we will hear further. Jethro was the son of Peter and married Mary Gardner, daughter of John Gardner, a third family responsible for an army of descendants and closely interwoven with the romantic story of the island. This house was built for Jethro and Mary in 1686.

The shallow entry leads to the two main rooms and its boxed-in stairs conduct to the two chambers on the second floor. Each front room has a large fireplace and there is one in the lean-to, drawing through the same chimney. The room at the right of the entry was the living room and that at the left the "Parlor," while the cooking and also the eating were done in the lean-to kitchen. The front rooms are large square chambers, and those on the second floor of equal floor space with a single window each and a fireplace but little smaller than the first floor. This house has no studding, the second floor and roof resting on the heavy girths, eleven inches square, and these in turn supported by equally heavy posts. The floor is upheld by a summer at right angles to the chimney resting on the girths. The summers are of pine ten inches square while the chimney jamb is fourteen inches square. Ship's knees, *i.e.*, brackets of the kind used in ships, are now in use at the corners but these have been substituted for the original corner posts as the latter became defective.

This house is one of the few of the old houses which has not been remodeled to meet changing styles and in its general lines, allowing for reshingling, larger windows, etc., undoubtedly conforms very nearly to the original. The inverted U on the chimney, the real significance of which has never been explained, is responsible for its name among the townsfolk as the "Horse Shoe House."

An interesting comparison with this Coffin home is found in the Mary Griswold house of Guilford, Connecticut. The lines of the two houses are almost identical, the Guilford house having a slightly longer front roof and a stone chimney as compared with brick in Nantucket. The Griswold

The Mary Griswold House. Guilford, Conn.

house was built in 1793, one hundred and seven years later than the Coffin house and illustrates the persistence of this early type in the spiritual republic of New Haven, the most conservative of all the colonies. Its present owner, now ninety years old, is of the third generation of the family of the original builder.

The Seth Coffin house of Nantucket is a good illustration

of the original method of building a single room in width
with chimney at end, the chimney, however, not a part of
the end wall and not exposed as in the Waite-Potter and
James Greene houses. This house was built in 1729 and its
exterior has been considerably modernized as shown in the

The Seth Coffin House.   Nantucket.

photograph. It still has, however, its shallow entry and stairs
rising steeply against the chimney, and the summer posts
and girths are all plainly to be seen in the rooms though
papered over and painted. This plan provided but one main
room on each floor and was at an early date superseded by
the double two story house with chimney and entrance in
the center, many examples of which will be seen later.

At a period earlier than the Jethro Coffin house, in Massachusetts Bay and Connecticut, a style of building had developed for dwellings of a more substantial character intended for the use of a pastor and his family or for the larger land owner or military leader of a district, which became

The Parson Capen House. Topsfield, Mass.

well-nigh universal toward the end of the XVIIth century and the beginning of the XVIIIth century. Many excellent examples remain and many variations closely approximating the type are included in our survey.

In this type the one room, one story house has expanded upward to two stories and laterally to two rooms. As a result we have the completed oblong two story and attic house with central chimney, steep roof and overhangs shown in the illustration of the Parson Capen house of Topsfield, Massachusetts.

This house in England would have had half-timbered construction for the walls. The overhangs, drops and brackets, which are for decoration purely, have their origin also in the mediaeval English type. In every line, in fact, the building bespeaks its English origin.

As was the case with most of the old houses, this faces south and is delightfully located on a knoll near the church just off the village green. It was built in 1683 by Parson Joseph Capen, soon after his arrival at Topsfield, for his bride, a daughter of the well known Appleton family of Ipswich. He and his wife lie side by side nearby, while his homestead remains to tell us the simple story of their lives.

The restoration of the old house has been sympathetically accomplished by Mr. George Francis Dow, Secretary of the Topsfield Historical Society, whose headquarters it has become.

As is evident from the construction, the house boasts four large rooms and a long attic. As in the case of other houses described, the huge chimney provides the four large fireplaces. The shallow entry, the narrow stair against the chimney and studded door are all characteristic of the time. The right-hand room is the "Hall" in which the family cooked, ate and spent their daylight hours. At the left is the "Parlor" intended for visitors and formal occasions. The custom was usually to have a four-post bedstead in this room. Over the Parlor was the "Parlor chamber" the best room, for the parents, while the rest of the flock were

The East End of the Parson Capen House. Topsfield, Mass.

The Parson Capen House. Topsfield.
Entry, Stairway and Door.

provided in the Hall chamber with four posters, trundle beds or cradles as their ages required. The attic also was a useful adjunct for growing families.

The Parlor has two summers, not a common feature. At one end of these timbers the date of raising the house is inscribed, namely, "July ye 8th, 1683." In the Hall fireplace is the brick oven with its door at the right and a niche said to be for pipes and tobacco. The illustrations are of the restoration of this room in the American wing of the Metropolitan Museum of Art, New York City. The original details have been faithfully copied and an excellent example of the XVIIth century New England living room is thus made available to students. The walls are paneled with wide pine boards simply moulded while the Parlor is plastered. There is a cellar at one side of the chimney and a half cellar at the other, both reached by trap doors through the floors.

The Capen house has no lean-to and the house of similar construction with the lean-to added is the logical sequence. An example of this sequence is found in the John Whipple house of Ipswich. The west end of this old mansion, that is, the left end of the south front shown in the first photograph, is the oldest. It is believed by Mr. Waters, the very conservative local historian, to have been built before 1638 and to be identical with the house of John Fawn to whom the lot was originally granted and who disposed of it in that year when he left to reside in Haverhill. From extant records describing the method of building in Ipswich the architectural evidence is in favor of that date. If this surmise is correct this is one of the oldest buildings standing in New England. In any case it may safely be concluded that the more elaborate east rooms with their carved oak

The "Hall" Fireplace. The Parson Capen House. From the
restoration in the Metropolitan Museum of Art, New
York City.

summers and heavy girth, providing the moulded overhang shown in the photograph of the east end, were added
by the son, Captain John Whipple some time between the
close of King Philip's War, 1677, in which he led a company
from Ipswich, and his death in 1683.

The John Whipple House. Ipswich, Mass.

The original building then was the west end with a chimney about where the present chimney stands, including the
present door and stairway. There were but two large rooms
possibly divided by partitions but the evidence of its ancient lineage is found in the long studs running up the two
stories from sill to plate, the second floor joists being supported by "side bearers" let into the studs and themselves

East End of the John Whipple House. Ipswich, Mass.

supported by a second set of studs. Into these studs are mortised two-inch, oak planks in the manner of building recorded for the earlier date. This was the period also of wooden chimneys and it is possible that the original chimney was of wood.

The lean-to attached to the west end only was undoubtedly added by the elder Whipple to provide for the needs of his increasing family, while, as already stated, the additional east half with the present chimney were erected by his son, the captain, about 1680, thus completing a typical single-chimney, four-room and lean-to house of the close of the XVIIth century. This house was appraised by the executors of the will of Captain John with two and a half acres of land, kiln and outhouse at £330, a very high valuation for that day. It is evident that this, as well as the Topsfield house of Parson Capen were much above the ordinary dwelling of the period.

The Whipple house has also been restored but a large part of the clapboards are original showing the hand-wrought nails, while the window openings and the heavy overhangs with brackets are provided for in the plan of construction. The sweep of the rear roof, not clearly shown in the photograph on account of the intervening foliage, adds a harmonious line to the main roof somewhat less steep than that of Topsfield. The chimney is less pilastered than the Topsfield chimney but has that sturdy size and squareness which is essentially characteristic of the Puritan home. From every angle the old house in its simplicity and harmony of line is a joy to the eye and expresses a like simplicity of thought and uprightness of purpose in its builders.

As one enters, the stairway to the second floor across the

shallow entry is faced and the Hall or kitchen is on the right. In the illustration the width of the fireplace indicates the size of the chimney foundation which provides not only for this but for another fireplace of similar size in the Parlor. At the right end of this fireplace is the brick oven and to the

The "Hall" of the John Whipple House. Ipswich, Mass.

right of it, is the built-in cupboard, an almost invariable accessory to these old fireplaces. The size of the chimney jamb, girths and summer with its transverse is to be noted. These are all of oak, hewn and chamfered by hand. The walls are paneled. The furniture is that of the period even to the table cloth of domestic linen woven on some family hand loom. The table service includes the pewter, the old

English porcelain and the curved knives and spoons, as forks were not generally used until the XVIIIth century.

Mounting the stairs, the room on the left is the Parlor chamber. In this room the illustration shows the wide fireplace opening with its simple hand-tooled moulding with-

The "*Parlor chamber*" of the *John Whipple House. Ipswich, Mass.*

out mantel. It was well along in the XVIIIth century before mantels were generally adopted. The chamfered summer is here, it will be noted, parallel to the chimney. The chimney wall is, as in practically all of the old houses, paneled with wide pine boards, simply moulded and unpainted. The floors also are of similar boards sometimes as wide as twenty-four inches. Visitors marvel at the width of these boards but fail to note that most of them contain the heart of the tree, indicating that the log was sliced through from bark to bark and not "canted" as is the modern custom to get the most out of the log. The old method was the only one possible in the day of a hand saw with a man at each end, but a wasteful system and one not to be emulated. The same system of sawing may be seen in operation in China today.

This old Whipple house, now the home of the Ipswich Historical Society, is redolent of memories of many generations. The lot on which it stands was one of the first distributed on the establishment of Ipswich in 1634. Next to it was the lot of Mr. Denison, the military leader, and later the Major General of the colony, on which he built his house. The first John Whipple was a man of education and some property as the prefix of "Mr." to his name rather than the usual title of "Goodman" indicates. He was from all accounts a leader in all the town's affairs and of an uprightness and a piety which merited such leadership. He rose through all the grades of progress in the community and was in turn "Freeman," deputy to the General Court at Boston and one of the Selectmen of his town. During most of this time he was "Deacon" also but his crowning honor came in 1658 when he was made ruling Elder of the church with a seat just a little lower than the Minister's.

In his lifetime he was a close friend of all the leaders of his day, beloved by all about him as instanced by the frequent references to "our Deacon," active in affairs of church and state, his house the meeting place of the men and women of the time who were laying the foundations of the self-governing communities of the future.

John Whipple left one son, John, and four daughters of whom the youngest was Sarah who married when she was twenty Joseph Goodhue, the son of Deacon William Goodhue. Sarah was the mother of ten children and the marriage was an unusually happy one.

Of the many documents in existence illustrating the spiritual background, the singleness of purpose and the devotion to the members of the family group, which characterized the Puritans of that day, none is more touching, none breathes more deeply the conviction of human frailty and divine blessedness than the "Valedictory and Monitory of Sarah Goodhue"[1] left in anticipation of her passing at the birth of her last child.

She addresses herself first: "Honoured and most loving father and mother, I cannot tell how to express your fatherly and motherly love toward me and mine . . . for the which in poor requital I give you hearty and humble thanks. . . . Be not troubled for the loss of an unworthy daughter; but rejoice in the free grace of God that there is hopes of rejoicing together hereafter in the place of everlasting joy and blessedness."

She then admonishes her brothers and sisters against "that swift and sudden messenger . . . that no one of you may be found without a wedding garment." To her children she leaves some pages of excellent advice beginning: "O my children all, which in pains and care have cost me dear: . . . be sure to set the fear of God before your eyes, consider what you are by nature, miserable sinners, utterly lost and undone; and that there is no way and means whereby you can come out of this miserable estate but by the mediation

[1] Ipswich in the Massachusetts Bay Colony, by Thos. F. Waters.

of the Lord Jesus Christ," and later she adds: "My children, in your life and conversation, live godly, walk soberly, modestly and innocently: be diligent and be not hasty to follow new fashions and the pride of life that now too much abounds. Let not pride betray the good of your immortal souls."

Most touching of all is her last address: "Dear Husband, I can do no less than turn to thee and if I could I would naturally mourn with thee . . . A tender hearted, affectionate and entire loving husband thou has been to me several ways. . . . This twenty years of experience of thy love to me in this kind, hath so instamped it upon my mind, that I do think that there never was man more truly kind to a woman . . . was it not to this end that the Lord was pleased to enable thee and give thee in heart to take (as an instrument) so much pains for his glory and my eternal good, and that it might be thy comfort."

And after much more expression of the deep love she bore this husband, almost too intimate to repeat, she closes in this simple fashion:

"O dear heart, if I must leave thee and thine, here behind, of my eternal affection here is my heart and hand.

"Be courageous and on the living God bear up thy heart in so great a breach as this.

"Sarah Goodhue

"July ye 14th, 1681."

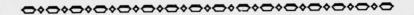

CHAPTER II

DEVELOPMENT OF THE NEW ENGLAND HOMESTEAD

(Continued)

T HE pioneers of England's empire, during the period we are considering, were with difficulty wrenching a precarious living from the reluctant soil of a New England, but in so doing were achieving, though with slow and painful steps, the expression of a community life, of an ideal of religious and political liberty, and establishing the individual home in its characteristic surroundings.

In France at the same time a program of building of unprecedented magnificence was in progress which culminated in the Palace at Versailles devoted to the glory of a monarch and to the pleasures of his court. Its extravagance, though it sowed the seeds of later catastrophe, at least gave the world the genius of Le Veau and of Mansard. The germ of this revival was working, though more slowly, across the Channel and manifested itself toward the end of the century in the masterpieces of Inigo Jones and Christopher Wren.

Throughout the old world this artistic and cultural leaven was at work expressing itself in an architectural revival which soon entirely superseded the Gothic tradition, and finally took shape in England in its individual form called the Georgian or English classic.

In the new world the struggle for existence, as well as the more restrained and simpler fashions resulting from an austere outlook on life, postponed the acceptance of this more decorative school. It is natural that it should first manifest itself in that colony in which the Puritan ideal was weakest and last where the zeal for the Puritan ideal was most intense. Before 1720, therefore, as we shall see, excellent specimens of Georgian houses appear at Portsmouth, a center of trade, of seafaring and episcopacy, while not until well along towards the end of the XVIIIth century is the fashion adopted in the Republic of New Haven and even then in restrained form.

New England owes more perhaps to Christopher Wren than to any other for the inspiration of its architectural triumphs, yet the measure of its acceptance of this inspiration marks the measure also of the relaxation of the Puritan ideal. In our consideration of typical houses, therefore, several variations of the old tradition must intervene before the English classic appears.

We have seen in the Parson Capen house at Topsfield (Chapter I) the evolution of the rectangular two story, four room, single chimney house which followed the two-room, one story house and preceded the lean-to. This development, however, took place in earlier houses in a simpler, less decorated form, as shown in the John Alden house of Duxbury. This house was built in 1653 by Jonathan, the third son of John and Priscilla Alden. For twelve years or thereabouts both parents lived here and both died here and the little chamber off the kitchen is that shown as their last resting place. John was the youngest of the signers of the Mayflower Compact and the last to die. This

The John Alden House.   Duxbury, Mass.

house, therefore, is believed to be the only house standing actually occupied by a Mayflower pilgrim.

The farm on which the house was built was an original grant to John Alden and has remained since in the Alden family up to the eighth generation of John Aldens. It is not likely now ever to fall into alien or unsympathetic hands, since it has become the property of the Alden kindred who, each year at the time of the family reunion, make their annual pilgrimage from all parts of the country to this shrine.

A house was built in the next field in 1627 but was burned a few years later. Jonathan, it is understood, was not married when the house was built. His father undoubtedly aided in its raising as he was a cooper by trade and one of those who joined the Mayflower company at Southampton.

The exterior has been restored as is evident in the illustration but the simplicity of the original lines is maintained. The interior presents many of the typical ancient features such as the steep stair against the chimney, three large fireplaces on the first and two on the second floor. None of the original Alden furniture remains. The paneling was added early in the XVIIIth century.

Quite similar in line to the Alden house is the old John Dillingham place of West Brewster, Cape Cod, built in 1660. This is the typical two-story lean-to and is the Alden house duplicated with the lean-to added. It is more than likely that it originally was of the same rectangular plan and that the lean-to was built later. It also has been restored so far as the exterior is concerned but has the three large fireplaces on the ground floor and two on the second, with the shallow entry and stair in front of the chimney. The hand rail and trim of the stair date apparently from about 1725. The excellent but simple paneling in the Parlor and Hall are probably of like age.

The house has never changed ownership and is now the summer home of the seventh generation. The original

The John Dillingham House. West Brewster, Cape Cod. 1660.

John Dillingham was brought by his father to Lynn from England when he was three years of age. When he reached maturity he was granted a tract of land on the cape running from Bayside to Seaside and engaged there, in addition to his farming, in the evaporation of salt from sea water which was the prevailing industry of the district.

The direct evolution of the Dillingham lean-to is the Dillingham, square, two-story, hip-roof, single-chimney house next door. These two houses stand on the King's Highway, not a hundred yards apart. The latter was built about 1760 by the grandson of the first John Dillingham and it also has remained in the same family to the present time. The business of making salt was abandoned for seafaring

The Dillingham House. West Brewster, Cape Cod. 1760.

and in the early XIXth century this house became the home of the master of a clipper ship.

In this later dwelling expansion of the lean-to form is obtained by substituting the hip roof, allowing for two full stories of equal size with a rear ell. The central chimney, however, is retained while only in its exterior lines and in the beginnings of simple decoration of windows and door is the Georgian influence apparent.

Long before the date of this last house, along the north shore of Massachusetts Bay, the classic style had begun to dominate the building of fine dwellings. The English manor with the hip roof served as the model for many, particularly in the Piscataqua towns. In this type, as

The Wentworth-Gardner House. Portsmouth, N. H.

shown in the Wentworth-Gardner house of Portsmouth built in 1760, two chimneys between front and rear rooms are substituted for the single-chimney type. In point of development, this house is a combination of two center-chimney houses with a hallway between them. This permits the wide entrance hall running the full depth of the house with doors opening from it to the four large rooms on each floor.

The hall became the dominant feature of Georgian houses, and all the arts of the wood carver and the decorator were called upon, as greater wealth and a desire for elegance of living followed, to make this hallway a dignified and often a sumptuous introduction to the hospitality of the mansion.

Photograph by Paul J. Weber

The Wentworth-Gardner House.   Upper Hall.

Particularly does this dwelling represent the elegance and the taste of the Portsmouth of the pre-Revolutionary days.   Built by Madam Mark Hunting Wentworth for her son Thomas, it became in 1792 the residence of Major William Gardner who was an acting Commissary to the army during the Revolution and was appointed, as a reward for his services and sacrifices, Commissioner of Loans and Pension Agent by President Washington.

The front entrance is not original and the Jacobean scroll and pineapple, common to the houses of this period, have

Photograph by Paul J. Weber

The Wentworth-Gardner House. The Dining Room.

been substituted recently for a Victorian portico which was out of tune with the rest of the house.

The stairway in the Georgian house becomes an important feature as compared with its hard and narrow austerity against the chimneys of the primitive dwellings;

and in this Wentworth house the wood carver has elaborated it with a wealth of classic design. The high balustrade with spindles of four designs and its carved round newel post surrounded by four spindles all of excellent handwork

The Wentworth-Gardner House. The Stairway.

mark it as a fine specimen of the wood carving of the time in one of its most developed communities. The hallway is unusually wide with a heavy cornice of great elegance. Particularly fine is the landing window surmounted by the head of Queen Caroline carved in wood. All the classic orders are used in the designs of rooms and hallway on both floors. The fireplaces are large, bordered with Dutch tiles and surrounded by paneling of unusually beautiful effect, in many of them elaborately carved. The doors also are paneled in harmony, while the lines of the windows are brought easily to the floor by the built-in window seats. Entirely empty of furniture as these massive square rooms now are, they are not bare and are unusually satisfying to the eye.

The dining room has a rounded china closet and is decorated with an old French wall paper brought by Mr. Wallace Nutting from another old house when he was in possession of this mansion. The kitchen is very large with a huge fireplace and brick oven running to a third chimney in the rear ell. Opposite this fireplace is a built-in cabinet extending to the high ceiling. This fireplace and its accessories give one an excellent picture of the lavish hospitality of the period and the multitude of servitors necessary to carry on the family ménage.

From every point of view this house is an excellent specimen of its type and period. It is now the property of the Metropolitan Museum of Art of New York City.

As the square house with hip or gambrel roof took the place of the gable roof and lean-to, the earlier two-story houses located their two chimneys generally at the ends of the square structure. These two chimneys opposite the partition between front and rear rooms furnished two fireplaces each to the two rooms on each floor. This is shown in the Governor Smith house of Wiscasset. (See later.) From the two chimneys the next step was to the four chimney arrangement common to the more elaborate Georgian houses.

Fireplace.

This change to four chimneys may be seen in the Daniel Perkins Johnston house of Castine, Maine. Here each chimney furnishes its fireplace in each of the four rooms of both floors. The house is a simple, almost undecorated, specimen of the square two-story house with only rudimen-

The Daniel Perkins Johnston House. Castine, Me.

tary classic leanings in its side portico, unpretentious Palladian window and entrance doorway. (The lattice porch is a later addition.) It is painted yellow which has good precedent in colonial houses and is built of brick on the ends and of frame, with narrow clapboards, on the front. The house is interesting as marking a step from the old design and as illustrating the simple and harmonious lines in the

building of the smaller seafaring towns. It also illustrates
the very comfortable habit, common to many parts of New
England, of joining the barn to the house by a corridor woodshed which made it possible without exposure, to attend to
the needs of the stock in heavy weather. These out-build-

Stairway.   The Daniel Perkins Johnston House.

ings almost always, as here, assume a line in harmony with
that of the mansion. This house has also a very interesting stairway which rises from the middle of the hallway to
a landing where it separates into two parts both leading
to the hallway above. At the landing is a doorway which
opens on a similar landing in the rear hallway and from
this runs a similar stair to the rear door. The two stair-

ways, therefore, form a triangle whose apex is at the door.
The railing and spindles of mahogany, though light, are
solid. The whole stairway is a good example of the conscien-
tious handiwork of its time.

This house was built by Daniel Perkins Johnston in
1794 during the period of prosperity which followed the
Revolution. The original Daniel was Castine's first bank
president and his son Daniel was one of its distinguished
ship masters. Much trade ran in those days between Castine and New Orleans, and to the Gulf most of his voyages
led. The present owner is third in the direct line.

As the two-story, single-chimney, lean-to house may be
considered the typical home of the early period of New
England development so the gambrel-roof house became the
prevailing style during the middle period. The last quarter
of the XVIIth century saw many of the simple cottage
houses of this type in Plymouth colony and Connecticut
and rather later in other parts of New England. This
fashion of building grew in favor during the first quarter
of the XVIIIth century and by 1750 was the most characteristic style for both cottage and mansion,—not only in
New England but largely throughout the colonies. The
New England gambrel, however, differs somewhat from its
southern neighbors in that its two slopes are of about equal
width and medium pitch, while those of the middle colonies
are marked by a flatter pitch and a wider lower slope.

The types of architecture we have been considering have
all been the direct outcome of English inheritance and
tradition, but the gambrel finds no counterpart in Britain,
and for its origin we must seek Continental inspiration.
This style is the evolution of the Mansard, adopted as

The William Harlow House. Plymouth, Mass.

the prevailing style in the France of Louis XIV by the greatest of his architects. The word gambrel is derived from the supposed resemblance of its line to the gambrel or hock of a horse.

The William Harlow house of Plymouth is an example of its early use. This, the second oldest house standing in Plymouth was built in 1677 after the close of King Philip's War, with timbers which, the local histories inform us, were taken from the fort on Burial Hill, abandoned when the fighting ceased. If this be true, the last remnants of the first structure which served as fort for the first fifty years and in the early days as meeting house, lie embedded in the framework of this cottage. It is now the property of the Plymouth Antiquarian Society.

Harlow came to Plymouth from Salem and rose to be Selectman and a man of importance in the colony. He was also Sergeant of the Plymouth Company. The records show the granting of a small "knole" of land near his "now" dwelling on which to build a house. That is to say, he already had a home nearby.

The central chimney is retained with two and often three fireplaces while the gambrel allows additional space in the attic. This house has the shallow entry common to the lean-to type and the stairway rises to the second floor straight from the door to a landing against the chimney from which it divides into two branches.

The Peter Toppan house of Newbury, Mass., 1697, shows the development from the one-and-a-half story to the two-and-a-half story gambrel with central chimney. The house as it stands includes two original houses joined together, each with its chimney and separate entrance.

The present owner has substituted the single front door shown in the illustration and has thrown the two houses together. The shallow entry and steep stair against the chimney remind us of the lean-to houses. There are fireplaces on both floors with framing similar to the lean-to type.

The Peter Toppan House. Newbury, Mass.

The middle section of the front was originally of narrow clapboards.

Near where this house stands, at the "Trayneing Green" just south of it, three companies of riflemen under Captain Morgan encamped in September, 1775, as part of the expedition to capture Quebec of which the moving spirit was Colonel Benedict Arnold. On the 19th of that month one thousand men embarked in ten transports at this point and set sail for the mouth of the Kennebec River.

In the early days of the XVIIIth century Portsmouth was a community of greater wealth than that of its neighbors. Settled by the followers of Mason and Gorges under Royal Charter, following prevailing middle-class sentiment in England and restricted by no rigidity of religious belief, its early citizens came frankly to the new world as a business venture, to trade in furs with the Indians, to barter in fish and to engage in shipping between the mother country and the colonies. They were town dwellers and in their better building early adopted the square, three-story, compact house of the English towns. And so in the Warner house, built between 1718 and 1723, we find a developed early Georgian type, at a time when in Massachusetts and Connecticut the building still followed the primitive and Elizabethan tradition.

This house was built by Captain Archibald MacPheadris, a Scotchman, a prominent merchant and King's councillor in 1722. It is believed to have been the most elaborate residence in New England at that time. Its walls, eighteen inches thick, were built of brick imported from Holland. The five years required for its construction and its cost— £6000, a large price for a residence of that day,—mark it as well in advance of contemporary building. It has three chimneys, a plan used often in later buildings, two at one end and one at the other. The hall is frescoed in most unusual fashion and, as a matter of historic interest, the lightning rod on the west end is said to have been installed under the direction of Dr. Benjamin Franklin in 1762 and probably to have been the first in New England.

The daughter of Captain MacPheadris married the Hon. Jonathan Warner who was King's Councillor until the Revolution. This fact accounts for the name now given to the house.

From the middle of the XVIIIth century, larger and more commodious dwellings began to be the order of the day and

The Warner House.   Portsmouth, N. H.

many were built with the gambrel as their main feature with an increasing amount of decoration of the simpler classic orders. At this time Georgian architecture was becoming more prevalent in England. In New England the carpenters were beginning to use books of measured drawings, such as those of Ashur Benjamin, and book architecture,— that is, a system of rules deduced from old models,—is re-

sponsible for the building which followed up to and after the
Revolution.

In the Governor Bradford house of Bristol, R. I., the
gambrel is used with the dormers and two-end chimneys,
common to pre-Revolutionary gambrel houses. The gam-

The Governor Bradford House. Bristol, R. I.

brel varies from the more typical New England design in
that the upper slopes are narrower than the lower.

This mansion was built before the Revolution and was
one of the few buildings which escaped destruction when
the British sacked Bristol in 1778. The residence of William Bradford, at that time Deputy Governor of Rhode Island, located on the main street, was burned and this

loss caused him to buy in 1781 the mansion we are considering.

The career of this William Bradford, born at Plymouth in 1729 and fifth in descent from the historian of the Mayflower, illustrates the virility of the stock and the indomitable energy which rose to meet the extraordinary demands of that vivid period.

He was educated first as a doctor, moved to Warren, R. I. and later to Bristol where he practiced his profession successfully. Later he took up the law and became eminent in both professions. In this, to us, extraordinary combination, his career paralleled that of Judge Holten of Danvers.

In 1761 he was first chosen to represent his town in the General Assembly and from that time was influential in all affairs of his state until his death in 1808. At the outbreak of the Revolution he was member of the General Assembly and was sent as a delegate to the Continental Congress. When the Colonial Governor Wanton was deposed and Deputy Governor Cooke replaced him, Bradford was made deputy. After 1778 he was continued as representative of Bristol in the General Assembly until he was elected senator of the United States for Rhode Island. For eighteen years he was speaker of the House of Representatives of the Colony and State of Rhode Island and for thirty-five years represented Bristol in the General Assembly.

In the next four houses we reach the apogee of the Georgian style as the culmination of colonial and early national architecture in New England. Marked by greater elegance of finish and richness of decoration, they represent the period of accumulated wealth and culture which springs from increased leisure.

The Governor Smith house of Wiscasset, Maine, so called
from having been the residence of the third governor of the
state of Maine, was built in 1792 by Silas Lee, a lawyer, and
is still owned by the third generation of this family. It
represents the two story type, hip roof in which the harmony

The Governor Smith House. Wiscasset, Me.

of design is enriched with the simpler classic orders. The
walk on the roof, a sailor's outfit, suggests the seafaring
inclinations of the town. It was in this house that that
charming and delightful classic of the last generation "One
Summer" was written by Blanche Willis Howard.

The Hamilton house of South Berwick, Maine, three
stories with four corner chimneys and Georgian dormers

represents a larger development of the same type. It was
built shortly before the Revolution by Jonathan Hamilton,
a West Indian trader. While it is now over the line in the
State of Maine, it is located on a promontory jutting into
the Piscataqua, now the Salmon Falls River but fifteen

The Hamilton House.   South Berwick, Me.

miles above Portsmouth and near the head of navigation.
The West Indian ships came up the river and unloaded and
reloaded their cargoes on this point. The original landing
was on the end of the point from which a path rose through
a terraced garden to the west entrance. The location of the
house, on the crown of the point overlooking the wooded bay
into which the river here widens, is extraordinarily beautiful.

Both exterior and interior have been somewhat altered by the present owner to meet modern conditions but wholly within the spirit of the period.

The broad central hall is flanked by a large drawing room on the west side with a small room in the rear recently added, and on the east side by a dignified and spacious dining room obtained by throwing a narrow hallway and stair of the original plan into the main room. The woodwork in both of these rooms is original. A peculiarity of the finish is that the rooms on both first and second floors of the west side have mantels of the usual Georgian style while the rooms at the east end have none. The drawing room is paneled about the fireplace, with unusually good carving, as is the dining room. The chambers are simpler. The staircase is a handsome example of the time though not as elaborate as that of the Wentworth-Gardner house.

The present owner has had a reproduction made of the wall paper in the hallway, of which fragments remained. The drawing room and dining room are frescoed over paper by an American artist in the scenic style of the period, using, however, New England scenes and buildings of the XVIIIth century, as a background. The drawing room is in tones of green and the dining room in tones of blue. The effect is delightful. The kitchen retains its very fine large fireplace with bake oven.

Jonathan Hamilton was a well-known man of his time. When John Paul Jones was fitting out the *Ranger* at Kittery across the river from Portsmouth, he recruited many of his sailors from the countryside about South Berwick and is reported to have been entertained many times in this mansion.

The end of the XVIIIth century brought to light in America several men of outstanding architectural ability. The best known of these is perhaps Charles Bulfinch, architect of the State House in Boston, the old State House in Hartford and many other public buildings in New England. More of the ancient craftsman school was Samuel McIntyre of Salem, wood carver and architect. He was the bright particular star of a family of joiners and wood carvers and came to be the most eminent architect of his district whose architectural development he controlled during his life which ended in 1811. He has not left us an original school of architecture but rather artistic perfection of detail applied to existing types. He found in Salem the three-story, square frame house the prevailing fashion of the pre-Revolutionary period. This was true also of Newburyport, Portsmouth and other towns of the north shore, and to a lesser degree of Providence. This square solid pile, not of any particular architectural value in itself, he embellished with pilastered corners, elaborate cornices, doors and porticoes, decked roofs and a wealth of classic detail for both interior and exterior. His ornamentation is all handwork taken from original classic models, not copied from earlier contemporary work. This elaboration of treatment satisfied the desire for elegance in the rich merchants who were then the rule in Salem, while the square mansion with the invariable garden at the back, made possible the hospitality for which the port was noted.

The Pierce-Johonnot-Nichols house of 80 Federal St., built in 1782 is called the highest achievement of Samuel McIntyre and is generally considered the best wooden house of its period and type in New England. The interior woodwork was not completed until 1801. To be noted are a greater depth and width than in most houses of the time. The foreshortened third-story windows help to disguise the height of the building and add much to the architectural effect. The Doric order is handled throughout with con-

The Pierce-Johonnot-Nichols House. Salem, Mass.

summate skill. The urns on the gate posts are original but the posts themselves have been restored. The decked roof and belvedere added greatly to the beauty of the whole and offered the family the opportunity to sight the incoming ships down the bay when the occasion offered. In the rear a touch of picturesqueness is found in the brick paved court surrounded by stables and other outhouses.

From the porch a path led directly to the North River where the master's ships arrived from the Orient and discharged their cargoes.

This mansion was built for Jonathan Pierce, wealthy East India merchant of that prosperous period for shipping which followed the Revolution. He and his son-in-law, George Nichols, lost their fortune in 1826 and in 1827 the house was sold to George Johonnot, friend of both families. In 1839 the Johonnots died and bequeathed the house to George Nichols and his wife in trust for their four daughters. It is now owned by the Essex Institute.

In the John Brown house of Providence, built in 1786, we have a veritable palace of a merchant prince and perhaps the finest specimen of the three-story, square, brick Georgian mansion in New England.

The original ancestor, Chad Brown, came over from England in 1638 with his wife Elizabeth and their children but finding the religious atmosphere of Massachusetts Bay irksome, removed to Providence where he contributed his abilities as a surveyor to the upbuilding of Roger Williams' young community. Four brothers of a later generation formed the firm of Nicholas Brown and Company to engage in mercantile business, and this firm became very prosperous. The John Brown for whom this house was built was the third of the four brothers and the house was designed by his brother Joseph who was also architect of the Market House and joint architect with James Sumner of the beautiful Baptist Meeting House. The bricks are said to have been brought in ballast from England in the firm's ships.

The mansion is an excellent example of the earlier English classic, the Palladian window, portico, foreshortened third-

The John Brown House. Providence, R. I.

floor windows, balustrade and heavy cornice, all enrich the harmonious effect yet are handled with restraint.

At the time the house was built, John Brown was known as the richest merchant of Providence. At his own expense he cut a passage through the hill lying between his house and his wharves and even constructed a bridge which shortened the route to Newport by a mile and on this bridge he erected a statue of Napoleon for whom he had a great admiration. He was also responsible for the *George Washington*, the first ship to sail from Providence to the East Indies.

All four of the brothers were active in the establishment of Brown University, while the son of Nicholas was trustee, treasurer and chairman of the Board of Fellows for fifty years and its most munificent benefactor. This house was the center of social activity for many years. In it were given many of the Commencement dinners. George Washington was many times a guest. John Brown supported to his utmost the union of the states and served for two years in Congress. His most notable claim to fame, however, lies in his leadership in the famous plot which resulted in the destruction of H. M. S. *Gaspée* the first blood of the Revolution.

The British armed schooner *Gaspée* was stationed at Narragansett Bay to prevent smuggling. In the carrying out of his orders, the Commander, Lieut. Duddington, had been needlessly severe and he and his vessel had, as a result, become extremely unpopular up and down the Bay. On the ninth of June, 1772, while pursuing the sloop *Hannah*, sailing from New York to Providence, the *Gaspée* ran aground on Namquitt, since called Gaspée Point. The *Hannah* however escaped damage and safely docked at Providence. The news of the dilemma of the *Gaspée* spread like wildfire. A drummer marched through the streets calling for volunteers to seize the British ship before she could be floated at high tide. They were asked to meet at the house of Joseph Sabin on South Main Street. Eight long boats supplied by John Brown started down the Bay after 10 P. M. When nearing the point on which the *Gaspée* lay, they were joined by another boat from Bristol, Captain Simeon Potter in command. They were seen at once and fired upon, to which the attackers replied by promptly boarding the vessel. After a short fight, in which the commander was severely wounded, the crew were bound and set on shore while the vessel was burned.

Those who participated in this adventure made no secret of it, in fact it was a common boast about town and although £1000 was offered for information, no one was ever brought to trial.

CHAPTER III

THE ESSENCE OF PURITANISM

HE Pilgrims, as they had begun to call themselves when they had landed on the soil of the Netherlands, followed literally the Paulist injunction, "Wherefore, come out from among them and be ye separate . . . and touch not the unclean thing." To the end of separating themselves from that which they could not purify, they entered into a covenant of the Lord before they left England, by which they joined themselves "in the fellowship of the Gospel to walk in all His ways made known, or to be made known unto them, according to their best endeavors, whatsoever it should cost them." Pursuing further the guidance given them, they mutually agreed in the Compact signed in the cabin of the *Mayflower* that their purposes were: "For the glorie of God and advancement of the Christian faith and honor of our King and countrie" and that we "covenant and combine ourselves together into a civill body politick, for our better ordering and preservation and furtherance of the ends aforesaid: . . . to enact such just and equall laws as shall be thought most meete and convenient for the general good of the Colonie unto which we promise all due submission and obedience."

The power of a right idea accepted with conviction is shown in the progress which followed from this beginning. The suffering and the obstacles might have vanquished less ardent spirits, but their eyes, always on Heaven, their pains became but the chastening which prepared them for a higher destiny. In spite of the loss of half of their number in the first winter, the forty-nine left instituted and carried out, with Massasoit, and his braves, a three-day Thanksgiving after the harvest. In so doing they established a feast which a nation of a hundred million, three hundred years later, honors them by observing. By 1624 their success was assured and by 1633 they had repaid their borrowings from the Merchant Adventurers. In 1643 the population of Plymouth Colony had reached at least three thousand while she had become the parent of a plantation to the north already larger in population and richer in worldly goods than she.

The names of William Brewster, postmaster of Scrooby, William Bradford of Austerfield, Edward Winslow, John Carver, who early made the great sacrifice, and Miles Standish come to us as we follow the Pageant of the governor and his company when each Friday afternoon in summer, at the beat of the drum, they made their solemn pilgrimage to Burial Hill. We join with them in singing the old hymn:

"Dim grew the forest path, onward they trod;
Firm beat their noble hearts, trusting in God.
Grey men and blooming maids, high rose their song;
Hear it sweep, clear and deep, ever along.

" Pilgrims and wanderers, hither we come:
Where the free dare to be—this is our home."

And not less do we think of Pastor John Robinson, left behind in Leyden, to whom the Pilgrims owed so much of inspiration and wise counsel.

A few old houses of the Plymouth colony remain to remind us that an essential feature of the Pilgrim plan was to establish a home as the unit of the community.

Miles Standish was the only trained soldier of the company and as such was of great value to the colony in organ-

The Alexander Standish House. Duxbury, Mass.

izing its defense and furnishing them the necessary military training but he was more than a soldier and became the community's frequent ambassador to their Indian allies and to neighboring colonies. His monument stands on Captain's Hill across the bay from old Plymouth. Below it, on the point, is the small gambrel cottage generally credited to Alexander, his son. It is believed that it was built in 1666 after the father's death. Timbers from some earlier structure, possibly from the house of Miles Standish itself, were used in its construction as shown by the beams charred by their proximity to a fireplace which are still visible in the attic. The chimney and hearth are of imported English brick. The site of Miles' original house is placed at a rocky point about a quarter of a mile nearer Plymouth.

Between Captain's Hill and Plymouth and adjacent to the latter, lies the present town of Kingston which, until 1726, was an integral part of Plymouth. A short distance east of the Boston Post Road but concealed from it, stands, on a knoll, the Major John Bradford house. The western half was built in 1674 by John Bradford, grandson of the second governor and historian of the colony. As the house faces south, the older part is at the left of the illustration. The house is built on land which was originally part of the governor's estate. The east end was added between 1720 and 1740, the original house, therefore, was of two rooms, main chimney and lean-to. The framing indicates that the lean-to was built at the time of the original construction. The house was partially burned in King Philip's War.

The migrations of the manuscript of the "Narrative of the Beginnings of New Plymouth," by Governor Bradford, began in this house. This contemporary account, of inestimable value to historians, was written, it is believed, at the governor's home, which was located on the Jones River not far from the present John Bradford house. When he died, the manuscript was left to his son, the father of the builder, and is known to have been in this house between the years 1704 and 1728. Major Bradford loaned the precious document to Judge Sewall. The latter did not return

The Major John Bradford House.   Kingston, Mass.

it, but loaned it in turn to Thomas Prince. After various peregrinations it was finally landed intact in the library of the Bishop of London at Fulham. In 1897 the Consistory Court of the Diocese of London returned the manuscript to the Commonwealth of Massachusetts and it now reposes in the State House in Boston.

The old house is now owned by the Jones River Club which is carrying on in it a manufacture of hand-woven linen table covers and rugs. Its simplicity and harmonious lines are enhanced by its location on the hill, above the cross-road, and by the copse of trees which surrounds it.

The outer wall of the original house may be seen just within the doorway. The chimney was rebuilt when the addition was made, and the paneling restored. There is an interesting and very marked contrast between the old rooms showing the cross-summers and other early features and the newer rooms with their tiles and panels.

The Winslow house at Marshfield, a few miles north, is of somewhat later date and greater pretensions. It was built after 1699 by Isaac Winslow, son of Governor Josiah and Penelope Winslow and grandson of Governor Edward Winslow of the *Mayflower*. The present house marks the site of the Careswell estate, the home of Governor Edward Winslow, and is the successor of the first house, which was burned in 1699. During the following four generations it played an important part in the social and political life of the colony. General Isaac, the builder, was military commander of the colony and John Winslow, his son, a major general in the King's army. The latter was sent to Grand Pré to remove the Acadians from that country. This irksome task he is reported to have discharged with judgment and mercy. It is known that he brought many of the Acadians back with him to Marshfield.

The Winslows were all strong loyalists and the house became a Tory stronghold. During the Revolution a company of British troops was quartered here. Dr. Isaac Win-

The Winslow House. Marshfield, Mass.

slow, son of the general, was a man of distinction and the last Winslow to reside in the house. In 1830, Daniel Webster, whose estate adjoined, bought the property. After his death it came into the hands of the Webster Association and after being occupied by several tenants was purchased by the "Historic Winslow House Association." Here each year the Winslow clan gathers from all parts of the country.

The front section is the original house and the ell directly back of it was built about twenty-five years later. The barn, seen at the left of the illustration, is original and has been moved to its present location and joined to the rear of the old building by a modern corridor, now used as a tea room.

The house is notable for its high studding and an entrance hall deeper than is customary, a high pitched roof and enclosed doorway. The windows are also wider than in other houses of the period. The framing was originally, exposed as was the habit, but General John remodeled part of the home when he returned from Grand Pré, leaving the parlor and kitchen as they were in the XVIIth century while the hall was paneled and tiled in the Georgian fashion. He is responsible also for the quoining of the exterior corners and the front entrance.

The very fine stairway runs to the second story and is of original XVIIth century-hand tooled pine.

Settlements along the north shore of Massachusetts Bay followed close upon the heels of Plymouth. It was only three years after the landing at Cape Cod that Roger Conant and his followers armed with the Sheffield patent, authorizing the settlement of the north shore, established an outpost at Cape Ann. The spot chosen, however, did not prove satisfactory and three years later in 1626 those who remained were glad to find shelter on a neck of land protected from the north winds by a high point which they called Naumkeag from the Indian tribe of the neighborhood.

In England the Puritans were chafing under the religious restrictions placed upon them by the Church of England

and were longing to emigrate to the new world in spite of the hardships their fellows were known to have undergone. And so two years later, they obtained a charter to the north shore which reserved the rights of the earlier colonists, and Captain John Endicott sailed with a party of settlers who assumed the leadership of the young community of Roger Conant and laid out streets and granted lands to new and original planters in what is now the center of Salem. "Salem" means peace yet peace was certainly not characteristic of the colony's first three-quarters of a century.

Endicott was the representative of "The Governor and Company of Massachusetts Bay in New England," and this became the official title of the colony. Rev. Francis Higginson, rector of a church in Leicestershire was the teacher and Rev. Samuel Skelton the first pastor of Salem. Both these men carried the M. A. of Cambridge University. In 1629, John Winthrop, a fine upstanding Puritan became governor and Thomas Dudley, his deputy. A year later, seventeen ships followed with a thousand Puritans who founded Boston and other towns. Many ex-clergymen of the Church of England were among these emigrants, including John Cotton, rector of St. Botolphs and Thomas Hooker and John Harvard of Emmanuel College, Oxford. The last, in 1638, left his library and one-half of his estate for a college in New England and this bequest with the addition of £400 voted by the General Court in 1636 established Harvard College. In honor of the mother university the name of the town in which it was located was changed from Newtown to Cambridge. In 1633, Ipswich was settled by the son of Governor Winthrop to forestall the French who were moving in that direction, and so by 1635 all along the shore as far as the Piscataqua, settlements were established which, for the moment, drew their inspiration and gave their fealty to Massachusetts Bay.

During this time religious differences arose which seriously threatened the existence of the church-state in the

House of Seven Gables. Salem, Mass.

new world. The Puritans, abhorring the corruption of the established church at home, saw the working of the devil in every individual who differed with them, and with relentless energy drove them from their midst. Of such were Roger Williams and the Antinomians of Mrs. Hutchinson, and it was the impulse of the same motive that produced the laws against the Quakers.

A distinguishing characteristic of many of the XVIIth century houses of Salem is the use of the gable roof in the style of the Elizabethan half-timbered manors either with or without dormers. This marked difference from the square, steep-roofed Parson Capen house of Topsfield and the

House of Seven Gables.   Salem, Mass.
North Front Facing Garden.

Whipple house of Ipswich, is shown in the two views of the House of Seven Gables. Built in 1669 by John Turner, the third John sold it to Captain Samuel Ingersoll in 1782. Mrs. Ingersoll was a Hawthorne. She left the house to her daughter, Susannah, a spinster, and Nathaniel Hawthorne was one of the few men allowed to cross her threshold. The house was gradually enlarged, the oldest part being the east end of the south side not shown in the illustrations. This has a lean-to on the east end of recent origin. Before 1891 the big chimney stack was removed and a fire-back disclosed, marked with the original date, 1669. In Hawthorne's time there were but five gables but Miss Ingersoll insisted that in earlier times it had seven. The architect when restoring the roof found, it is understood, the remains of rafters originally used for the extra gables and so made the necessary extension to provide them.

Through the generosity of Miss Caroline Emmerton of Salem, the complete restoration of Seven Gables was made possible in 1909. It is now used as a social settlement in the winter months. To the same grounds has also been moved and restored the "Old Bakery" formerly at 23 Washington St., built in 1683 by Benjamin Hooper. Between the two houses the garden, with its lawn extending to the water and its delightful outlook across the bay, offers hospitality and a friendly cup of tea to its many visitors. The chief interest of the house naturally lies in its connection with Hawthorne and his romance. Other stories by him also have a connection with it. Hawthorne lived in so many Salem houses and its ancient flavor had so much of inspiration for him that what is left of the older houses constantly suggest his presence. From the "Town Pump" to the "Scarlet Letter," Salem was often in his thoughts.

Up to a few years ago Salem was unique in possessing many of the XVIIth century Elizabethan gable-roofed houses. Most of them have, however, been destroyed or so mutilated as to be beyond recognition. One of the best specimens remaining is the restored John Ward house removed to the garden of the Essex Institute. This house, originally at 38 St. Peter's St. was built in 1684. In its former location it rested on the ground. It will be noted that it has a wider overhang than is usual, without drops. The overhang is also an Elizabethan inheritance. As found

The John Ward House. Salem, Mass.

in English Elizabethan houses it is sometimes wide enough to protect foot passengers from the rain. In America the use of this feature can be considered as intended for decoration purely and as part of the inherited tradition.

The descendant of the half-timbered, Elizabethan house is again seen in the John Pickering homestead, the oldest of the XVIIth century houses standing in Salem proper. The date given in the family records is 1651, though that stamped on the fire-back in the dining room is 1660.

With the exception of the entrance, which has been moved forward, the lines of the house are those of the original design, though the trim, fence etc., are part of extensive alterations made in 1841. Originally there was a lean-to but this rear roof has been raised to provide additional room. In the northeast room, the original "hall" the hand-hewn summer and gun-stock posts are exposed. In the "parlor" the summer is encased in paneling. The entrance hallway is most interesting with its original stairway against the chimney, the typical railing of the period and excellent paneling. The present owner, has cut through the brickwork of the original chimney a passage which now extends from the left of the hall stair to the dining room in the rear.

The first John Pickering, a craftsman by trade, built the house himself. With the three generations of John Pickerings now alive, ten generations of the family have continuously lived in this house. The most eminent of its sons is Timothy of Revolutionary fame. As a staff officer of General Washington he was present at the battles of Germantown and the Brandywine and was Postmaster General and later Secretary of State in the Cabinet of the president.

Danvers, though now a separate township, was originally and for many years a part of Salem. Its earliest houses are therefore equally witness to the history of colonial Salem. No more pathetic figure comes upon the scene of that early history than that of the revered and venerable mother of nine children so brutally dragged from the bosom of her family to a shameful death on the gallows.

The Rebecca Nourse house still stands in Danvers and in

1907 was purchased and restored by the Rebecca Nourse Memorial Association. It is known as the Townsend Bishop house and was built in 1636. It was in this house that Rebecca Nourse lived and from this house she was taken to her trial and to the gallows. Her monument and grave are

The John Pickering House.   Salem, Mass.

nearby, the former raised by her descendants in 1885. John Greenleaf Whittier wrote the inscription.

Rebecca Nourse was one of three daughters of William Towne of Yarmouth, England, all of whom were arrested, tried and executed as witches. At the time of her trial she was not only a mother but a grandmother of numerous grandchildren, her husband, a man of integrity and she herself, as John Fiske says "a model of every virtue." She was tried before Magistrate Hathorne who it is recorded, was in some doubt as to her guilt but his heart was hardened by the recurring fits of the girl accusers and the fact that she said little in her own defense. The jury first brought in a verdict

The Rebecca Nourse House.   Danvers, Mass.

of "not guilty."   But the Thursday lecture of the Rev. Deodad Lawson, following a visit from the deluded children, had plunged the community into a state of more intense madness; and the jury was sent back and practically charged to bring in a verdict of guilty.   They did so, with the result that this unoffending lady was excommunicated from the church and hanged on the gallows.

Cotton Mather, answering for the Boston ministers, the request of the court of Oyer and Terminer for their opinion, warned against the acceptance of "spectral" evidence and noted the effect on the accusers of the presence of the accused. If his advice had been followed no conviction would have

The Rebecca Nourse House. Danvers, Mass.
South Front.

ensued in this case, since the evidence of Elizabeth Hubbard and Mary Walcott, her accusers, was entirely "spectral."

It was in Salem itself that the awakening from this delusion, widespread in England as well as in the colonies, took place. It was not without its deep and far-reaching effect on those who participated in the trials as shown by the picture of the times in the diary of Judge Samuel Sewall who, himself, five years later, publicly acknowledged his shame and repentance in Old South Church.

In the Nourse house we have come back to the single chimney, lean-to type characteristic of most of the primitive

The Holten House. Danvers, Mass.

houses. Its interior is not only filled with interesting furniture and household utensils of the period but is an excellent specimen of the XVIIth century work.

In the Judge Samuel Holten house at Danvers we see the final product of three distinct periods joined in one harmonious whole. The original house, now represented by the middle three windows, chimney and steep roof was built by Benjamin Holten in 1650. To this square, two-story house was added first the lean-to and in 1752 the west (left-hand) end. At this time the three original fireplaces on the ground floor were bricked up. The east end and the ell were finally added after 1800 to furnish offices for Judge Holten. The small jut-out at the east end, a favorite device of the period and locality, is called hereabouts a "Beverly ell." Though somewhat bizarre in effect, it is often a convenient addition. The interior has lost many of its primitive features, though some remain, and has gained some excellent paneling as well as more spacious chambers. Judge or Dr. Samuel Holten achieved distinction in two professions as did Governor Bradford of Bristol, R. I., previously mentioned. First as a doctor of medicine he practiced successfully in Danvers and Gloucester. In 1768 he was elected to the General Court of Massachusetts and was representative in the Provincial Convention of 1768 and to the Provincial Congress of 1775 and the Yorktown Convention which framed the Constitution of the United States. He served five years in the Continental Congress, for a time as its president, two years in the Congress of the United States, five years in the Massachusetts Senate and twelve years on the Governor's Council. For thirty-five years he was judge of the Court of General Sessions of Essex County and fifteen years its chief justice. The mere catalogue of his activities is a sufficient indication, not only of the capacity of the man, but of the service expected of public servants in that formative period.

We have spoken of the origin of Cambridge. Of its many fine old houses the Deacon Cooper house of 21 Linnean St., built about 1657, is its best example extant of the XVIIth century. It is known that the deacon owned a house on the road to Menotomy opposite the Cow Common and this record appears to identify it with the house in question. Though not built on a road, a byway ran in front of it in 1725, at that time called "Love Lane," which was in time succeeded by the present Linnean St. The house was re-

The Deacon Cooper House. Cambridge, Mass.

stored in 1912 by the Society for the Preservation of New England Antiquities of Boston and is now owned by that society.

In its shape, oblong and rather shallow, and its pilastered chimney, it resembles the Parson Capen house of Topsfield but has a lean-to not shown in the photograph and but one overhang on the end gable. The type of window used in the restoration and the addition of the storm door adapt it for use under modern conditions. Its two ground floor rooms are excellent specimens of the period, with oak framing exposed and large fireplaces. The old barn stands in the rear and the original well is still in existence.

The Fairbanks House.   Dedham, Mass.

Of the many remaining houses of the colony of Massachusetts Bay there is none so well known and none has been so often pictured and described as the Old Fairbanks Home of Dedham. This is doubtless due to its picturesqueness, to its harmonious rambling line atop the knoll on which it stands and to the fact that but little restoration has been necessary to preserve it. As we pass around it and step in it, we find ourselves in the atmosphere of the XVIIth century pure and unalloyed. The old houses exude their personality and this one speaks of kindliness and peace. So well does it tell its own story that to dwell on the facts regarding it seems almost a supererogation.

It has not been the scene of events of historic import nor even a mansion of elegance or culture. A yeoman of old England, Jonathan Fayerbanke came with his family from England and built it in 1636. He chose Dedham which meant "contentment." He signed the covenant with eleven other persons to whom it was granted to establish this town and by which they agreed:

"We, whose names are hereunto subscribed, do, in the fear and reverence of our Almighty God, mutually and severally promise amongst ourselves and each to other to profess and practice one truth according to that most perfect rule, the foundation whereof is everlasting Love." Nor did they forget to add that most important adjunct to the Puritan faith: "That we shall by all means labor to keep off from us all such as are contrary minded . . ."

Its unique history lies in the fact that it has housed one single family only, that it has never been deeded, never mortgaged, but has grown gradually to such dimensions as we see without let or hindrance and that it has sheltered eight generations of the same family who have lived, raised their children and died in it, until the time of the three maiden daughters who brought its story to a close. And now it stands, a tale that is finished, with each year of its simple and peaceful progress written in the worn thresholds, and in the sagging rafters of its old rooms.

The Fairbanks family, now grown some twenty thousand

strong, still owns the place and wanders back singly and in clans each year, to renew their friendship with the old homestead. The original house, as is plainly seen in the illustration, is the middle portion with its chimney stack and lean-to. The east (right of front) gambrel addition was built about 1648 as the need of the family demanded and a few years later the west ell presumably for the use of the eldest son, John, and his family. The entire building, as it now stands, therefore, was completed well before the time of King Philip's War and fortunately escaped the general devastation of that period. The date of the original, 1636, seems to place it earlier than any other of the existing New England dwellings though several approximate this date.

In Concord, Massachusetts, the Hosmer House built by Governor Robert Winthrop in 1680 is an interesting central chimney lean-to house of the XVIIth century enlarged and adapted by a later generation.

This house stands on land originally granted Governor Winthrop who built for himself a house between this and the roadway at an earlier date. This latter house has disappeared except for the excavation for its cellar which remains to mark its location. The Hosmer house was sold first to a Mr. Hunt and by Hunt was transferred to Edmund Hosmer, descendant of James Hosmer, who is recorded in the State House, Boston, as one of the early emigrants. He was a man of unusual influence and a friend of the Rev. Peter Bulkeley, whom he had known in Cambridge, England. Charmed by the surroundings of Concord he chose to settle here and became one of its founders. It was his descendant, Edmund Hosmer, who bought the house in the XIXth century and gives it his name. It is still occupied by

Hosmer descendants. The original lean-to house is shown
at the right of the illustration. The ell with its end chimney was added a few years later. The oak framing is exposed in both wings of the house and the older portion
retains the original stair against the chimney. The parlor

The Hosmer House.   Concord, Mass.

in the ell is decorated with paper imported during the later
part of the XVIIIth century. It is the oldest house in Concord and contains many interesting relics.

A good three-story gambrel-roof house of the time is
the Foster house of Framingham near Dedham, built in
1693–4 by Jeremiah Pike, who became selectman and leader
in the community. This house also has remained in the same

family for eight generations. The present owner, last of
the direct line, plans to leave the house to a society which
will preserve it for posterity. Standing at a cross-road about
a quarter of a mile from the beautiful old green of Framingham, it is and always has been a farm house of a farm-

The Foster House. Framingham, Mass.

ing community, although industry existed, since, in the early
days, spinning wheels were manufactured in this locality.

The original Jonathan Pike was honored with the privilege of building a pew for himself in the Meeting house at
a time when the community largely sat on benches, in consideration of cutting a door through the end of said Meeting house by which his family might enter, an honor not

to be taken lightly or inadvisedly and one granted only to those in whom the community placed absolute confidence. His great-granddaughter, Mehitable, married Gideon Haven in Revolutionary times. The original commission from the Council of "Massachusetts Bay in New England" which constituted him in 1776 a second lieutenant in the Massachusetts contingent of the Continental Army is still in the possession of the family.

The last important exodus of Puritans from England, before the Long Parliament of 1640 brought this movement to a close, was that of John Davenport and his company who reached Boston in 1636. Two years later, after careful preparation had been made, the entire group which had come over from England were moved with their goods to the shore of Long Island Sound where, in 1638, the town of New Haven was founded. A year later saw Milford established and with new arrivals from England in 1640, Guilford followed. A little later Stamford was added and in 1643 the four towns were united in the Republic of New Haven. Brantford was shortly thereafter included and some of the colonists induced by reports from the Indians of the neighborhood, of the fertile land and good fishing, undertook to cross the Sound to eastern Long Island. The town of Southold was there established to be followed in turn by the settlement on the south shore of Southampton and Easthampton.

These were all part of the essentially Puritan movement which came directly from England for the purpose of founding its own ecclesiastical state in the new world. In this plan New Haven followed in the footsteps of Massachusetts Bay but without the Bay's practical experience of ten years it was even more rigid and less liberal. Davenport is called "the most extreme of revivalists." The vote in these new communities, therefore, was most strictly limited to those admitted to Communion in the church.

New Haven, then standing shoulder to shoulder with Massachusetts Bay, became one of the four colonies united in the Federation of New England from which Rhode Island was rigidly excluded. By 1650, however, the difficulties of the situation had begun to be felt in Massachusetts, where one-fifth only of the population could vote through membership in the church and where the increasing invasion of the Quakers was gradually weakening the church's control.

The final separation of church and government followed the visit to England of John Winthrop, the son of Massachusetts' governor, in the interest of Connecticut. His charm of manner and manifest integrity of purpose won him recognition without delay, and he brought back with him a liberal charter for Connecticut which placed New Haven under its rule and removed the ecclesiastical restriction as to voters. A similar charter was obtained for Rhode Island. This established, for these two colonies, a liberal and autonomous government which was not changed in any essential particulars until the Revolution.

Connecticut's early seat of education was first established at Saybrooke, in 1701, and moved to New Haven in 1716. It was christened Yale College in 1718 in honor of Elihu Yale, a merchant of London. The original founders were ten ministers of the church, several of whom were graduates of Harvard. This institution early became the seat of conservatism and manifested less opposition to the old doctrine than did its sister college.

The Thomas Morris House. Morris Cove, Conn.

If we look now for an expression in architecture of the period above outlined, we must seek it outside the large industrial centers. In New Haven we will find tablets marking the sites of the early houses, but the old landmarks themselves have been obliterated. On the campus itself the single XVIIIth century building left is so surrounded by the new Yale that its presence is scarcely felt. Fortunately, down the Bay, one splendid old mansion of the early days remains.

The Thomas Morris house of Solitary Cove or Morris Cove, as it is now called, is the definite successor of the Waite-Potter house of New Bedford and the James Greene house of Buttonwoods, R. I., previously described. The stone chimney built into the end wall, the main feature, combined with wood framing for the rest of the oblong gable-roof building. A repetition of this process is often seen in different parts of the same building and in the Morris Cove house it is repeated three times.

The date as given is 1671, at which time the oldest section, that shown in the center of the west front, was built. The second illustration shows the south end and chimney of the oldest part. The other two extensions were added in 1767. The end walls are of massive stone, in some parts of great thickness. There are eight fireplaces in all, two with Dutch ovens, also a long narrow vaulted ballroom with a huge kitchen underneath. Here the heavy oak beams are exposed.

The house was occupied by the Morris family for many generations. The original Thomas Morris chose the location presumably for its juxtaposition to ship timber and navigable water, since he was a shipbuilder and found his raw material back of the cove itself. He came with the Davenport company in 1638 and was one of the signers of the original plantation covenant. It was thirty years later that he bought this land and three years after that that he built his dwelling. In 1779, a British marauding expedition landed

The Thomas Morris House. Morris Cove, Conn.
South End.

on the east shore at Five Mile Point, looted the house and left it in flames. The fire was, however, extinguished before great damage was done. To mark the event a portrait of Amos Morris, showing the saber cuts of the vandal soldiery, still hangs on the wall.

A Morris descendant, Mr. William S. Pardee, purchased the mansion and restored it in 1915, and here he died in 1918.

The property has now been left to the New Haven Colony Historical Society with an endowment.

Guilford followed closely on the heels of New Haven with its founding in 1639, and in that year, as one of the founders, came the Rev. Henry Whitfield, pastor of the flock. By 1640 his residence, the most important in the town, was built, and remains to posterity as the "Old Stone House."

These end-chimney stone houses were comparatively common along the Connecticut shore, in southern Rhode Island and about New Bedford, but rare elsewhere in New England, though we shall see a very fine specimen in Newbury, Mass.

In contrast with New Haven, which has lost its old houses, Guilford is rich in XVIIth century and early XVIIIth century types. It has, in fact, at least one hundred houses standing of Revolutionary age or earlier. On Fair Street there are six in a row all built previous to or at the time of the Revolution and, in the "Old Stone House" or Whitfield house, it has preserved one of the most ancient stone houses in the United States.

This mansion was built both as a residence and a fort. It was probably somewhat smaller originally but is believed to have had three outside chimneys and tradition favors the single room running up the two stories as it has now been restored. Through many changes and two definite restorations, but little of the original remains. This little, however, seems plausibly to include the fine old chimney and north wall and most of the west wall and the general outline of both the front building and the ell. It is believed that the ell had originally an end chimney also similar to the main building. The last restoration took place in 1903–4 under

The Old Stone House. Guilford, Conn.

the supervision of Mr. Norman Isham of Providence as architect.

Closely associated with all of Guilford's history it now houses many of its most important historical relics. Henry Whitfield, for whom it was built, was a graduate of Oxford and an author. He had much to do with that early English missionary society called the "Society for the Propagation of the Gospel in New England" which still exists as the "New England Company" and carries on its work among the Canadian Indians. In the XVIIth century it supported John Eliot and his "praying Indians," so great a bone of contention during King Philip's War. At Henry Whitfield's death, his widow sold the property to Major Robert Thompson and it remained in his family until 1772 when it was sold to Wyllis Eliot of Guilford, great grandson of the Rev. John Eliot above mentioned. He promptly transferred it to Colonel William Pynchon, a loyalist who became a refugee. Colonel Pynchon managed to dispose of it in June 1776, a week before the Declaration of Independence, and its first occupant under the new order, strangely enough, was Samuel Griffing, a patriot refugee who had escaped from Southold, L. I., and had taken refuge in Guilford. And so the old mansion shared in all the vicissitudes of the changing conditions about it.

In 1900 it became the property of the state of Connecticut. The purchase and its establishment as a State Museum have been substantially assisted by the town of Guilford, residents of Guilford and members of the Colonial Dames of America.

In the Hyland house, Guilford's most typical XVIIth century house, we return to the familiar characteristics of the

John Whipple and similar houses elsewhere. John Hyland, the builder, came to Guilford in 1651 and it is presumed built the house soon after his arrival.

The single stone chimney has been restored above the roof, and the house, throughout, both interior and exterior,

The Hyland House. Guilford, Conn.

has been repaired and parts lacking have been restored, though always in harmony with the original. The overhang with its brackets indicates the more substantial home of the period. Its longer lean-to on the west end than on the east, added to internal evidence, incline one to the belief that it was built originally as an end-chimney, two-room house, the lean-to following and the east end added last.

Ebenezer Parmelee, the most interesting of its occupants, grandson of the builder, was a boat builder and mechanic. His contribution to the community was the old town clock. He built it in 1727 and from that time until thirty-five years ago, when the church was given an electric clock to take its

The Acadian House.   Guilford, Conn.

place, the old clock ticked away the hours in the church belfry recording the devotion and the skill of the craftsman who fashioned it.   It had but one hand, but that one was sufficiently accurate to meet the need of the peaceful old village until the motor bus and the trolley invaded its tranquillity. Its old mechanism now rests, covered with dust, in the attic of the Old Stone House.   With a touch the heavy pendulum starts again its accustomed labors, seeming to deny that it has outlived its day of usefulness.

The Acadian house, another of Guilford's primitives, resembles the Jethro Coffin house of Nantucket as a simpler product of that day marked by its single stone chimney, lean-to and its old windows and door.

The house is named from its having sheltered a family of Acadians who were put ashore here from a British ship in the autumn of 1755. Four hundred of the exiles were sent to Connecticut and billeted on the various towns. The use of this house for their shelter would indicate that they were received with kindliness and pity.

Joseph Clay, who came to Guilford from Saybrook in 1670, built the house.

One of the most charming of Guilford's older dwellings is the Comfort Starr house. Its oblong uprightness and gable overhang show the original two and a half story, single-chimney house, while the lean-to at a flatter angle than the roof is plainly of a later period. The main house is believed to have been built by Henry Kingsworth, who came from Kent, England, with the Rev. Henry Whitfield in 1639. It was sold to Comfort Starr with whose descendants it remained until 1874. Starr was a tailor and a great grandson of Dr. Comfort Starr who came from Ashford, Kent, to Boston in 1635. His tailor's goose remains and is now in the State Museum in the Old Stone House. That he used it to good advantage is shown by the fact that he died a rich man for those days.

Settlement of the eastern Long Island towns took place, as has already been mentioned, immediately after the founding of New Haven by John Davenport's company. The earliest English plantation was, however, that of Lion Gardner, the great man of the early period, at a point later called Easthampton in 1635. The eastern towns while nominally under New Haven actually were completely independent of each other and of outside control. They were,

The Comfort Starr House. Guilford, Conn.

in fact, pure democracies whose government was by town meeting, assembled by the beating of the drum. Every ordinance, so enacted, began: "It is ordered by the townsmen." By every tie of sympathy and friendship they were inclined to their Puritan brothers in Connecticut and Massachusetts Bay yet actually they were transferred to New York by Charles II. Dutch influence never reached the

east end. By the Hartford treaty of 1650 between Peter
Stuyvesant and Simon Bradstreet, Thomas Prince representing the United Colonies, the boundary between Dutch
and Connecticut control was drawn north and south from
the west end of Oyster Bay. Within ten years Stuyvesant
practically surrendered the largest part of Long Island to
Connecticut. The taking of New Amsterdam by the English
had therefore but little effect on the eastern towns. They
did, however, bitterly protest their transfer to the Duke of
York. In fact, Southold, Southampton and Easthampton
denied the right of King James to transfer their allegiance
without their consent and in 1671 Southampton filed her "re-
monstrance" and in the final treaty with Holland, Connecticut did her best to get the three eastern towns but without
success. With their brethren of New England the three towns
fought the exactions of the Andros tyranny twenty years later,
and in 1685 Easthampton, which had been settled by men from
Lynn, stood for "No taxation without representation," and
affirmed their birthright as free born Englishmen, for which
they were compelled to shed their blood a hundred years later.

Southold, though one of the earliest of the settlements,
has lost all its old landmarks. Southampton and Easthampton, however, particularly the latter, with its magnificent trees and beautiful green, still retain the charm of
the secluded New England village.

The two Easthampton houses illustrated, the John Henry
Mulford house and the John Howard Payne house both face
the village green and are the only XVIIth century houses
which remain standing. Both are apparently located on
property originally granted to Robert Dayton and this fixes
the date of both as before 1663. Both have the characteristics

of the early Massachusetts houses and particularly resemble the Nantucket and Cape Cod houses of the same period.

The present John Henry Mulford is the lineal descendant and the tenth of his line from the John Mulford of the original settlers, one of the first three justices of the court.

The John Henry Mulford House.   Easthampton, L. I.

The John Howard Payne house is famed as the home of the author of "Home Sweet Home." His father William Payne was master of English and writing in the Clinton Academy located then, as now, across the green from the house and for many years the son lived with him. The local histories tell us that John Howard was called, in early life, the American Roscius and that he was the author of

the tragedy of "Brutus" and "other dramatic compositions of high merit." Alas for fame! the dramatic compositions have failed to survive and the author is known for
the simple song of home which still appeals wherever the
spirit of the home exists. No lovelier setting could be found

The John Howard Payne House. Easthampton, L. I.

to move the poet than the simple old cottage, overhung
with honeysuckle, on the village green.

The Dr. John Mackie house of Southampton closely
resembles the Cape Cod type of cottage with its long sloping roof and central chimney. This house retains its shallow entry but the stair has been moved back of the living
room. Many other changes have been added to make it

more comfortable, but its harmonious lines remain to remind us of its British ancestry. Dr. John Mackie came to Southampton from Dundee, Scotland, in 1722. His house there, built of stone, is said to be still standing and this cottage to be an exact replica of it.

The John Mackie House.   Southampton, L. I.

The "Hollyhocks" of Southampton reminds us of the older Dillingham house of Cape Cod and the many Nantucket houses of this period.   It was built in 1660 either by Thomas Halsey, one of the original settlers, or his son Isaac and retains many of its original features.

Local history has it that it was in the doorway of an earlier house that Phoebe Halsey, the wife of Thomas, was tomahawked by a Pequot Indian in 1649, the first and practically the only casualty of the war in this locality.

The central chimney is brick above the garret floor and stone foundation. The stairway turns from left to right with baluster and spindles probably not original. Posts, girths

The "Hollyhocks." Southampton, L. I.

and summers are exposed both on first and second floors, the posts framed on a curved brace joining them to the girths, a "ship's knee," as is the custom at New Bedford and Nantucket.

The Rev. Abraham Pierson, a Yorkshire man, was the first pastor of the church at Southampton. He became a member of the church in Boston in 1640, and Cotton Mather records his opinion of him and incidentally gives us an inkling of the method of organizing these colonies of Puritan inclinations. He says: "Proceeding in their plantation they called Mr. Pierson to go with them who, with seven or eight more of their company regularly incorporated themselves into the church-state before going, the whole company entering at the same time with the advice of the Governor of Massachusetts Bay Colony into a civil combination for maintaining government among themselves. Thus was then settled a church at Southampton under the paternal care of that worthy man where he did with laudable diligence undergo two of the three hard labors, teaching and governing, to make it become what Paradise was called 'the Island of the Innocents.' It was afterwards found necessary for this church to be divided, upon which occasion Mr. Pierson referring his case to Council his removal was directed unto Brantford over upon the main and Mr. Fordham came to feed and serve that part of the flock which was left at Southampton; but wherever he came he shone. He left behind the character of a pious and prudent man and a true child of Abraham, now lodged in Abraham's bosom."

Mr. Pierson was of the John Davenport school in restricting the franchise to church members and was dissatisfied with the arrangements made with Connecticut in 1644. This was the reason for his removal to Brantford. Joined there by others from Wethersfield, Connecticut, of like inclinations, his second church for a time prospered, but though "worthy" he was uncompromising, and when Brantford came under Connecticut, he again removed with the more faithful of his flock, to the banks of the Passaic, where he founded Newark. His son, also the Rev. Abraham Pierson, was the first president of Yale College.

CHAPTER IV

THE FRONTIERS OF MASSACHUSETTS BAY

A PICTURE, drawn from life, of the labors of the pioneers in clearing the forests, planting their cornfields and their gardens, and in building their primitive shelters has come down to us in the "Wonder Working Providence of Sion's Saviour," by Captain Edward Johnson of Woburn.[1]

"The Winter's frost being extracted forth the Earth," he says, "they fall to tearing up the roots and bushes with their Howes even such men as scarce ever set hand to labour before, men of good birth and breeding but coming through the strength of Christ to war their warfare, readily rush through all difficulties."

Although Johnson wrote for the benefit of those left behind in England, it was as true of Massachusetts' northern frontier in 1633 as of his own settlement of four or five years earlier. Particularly were those who, with John Winthrop, Jr., made the journey from Boston to Agawam (Ipswich) in shallops in March of that year and shortly thereafter, "men of good birth and breeding." Among them were Governor Thomas Dudley with his two sons-in-law, Bradstreet and Denison, deputy and military leader. Also Symonds, deputy governor and Samuel Appleton of Waldingfield with his two

---

[1] "Wonder Working Providence of Sion's Saviour," by Edward Johnson of Woburn, edited by J. Franklin Jameson. Chas. Scribner's Sons, 1910.

sons, and Richard Saltonstall who built the first mill. These were all men of gentle families and from houses of distinction in old England.

Johnson explains the manner in which the primitive dwellings were built. "Now because it is one of the admirable acts of Christ's Providence in leading his people forth into these Western fields, in his providing huts for them to defend them from the bitter storms this place is subject to, therefore here is a short epitome of the manner how they placed down their dwellings in this Desert Wilderness". . . . "After they have thus found out a place of aboad, they burrow themselves in the Earth for their first shelter, under some hill-side, casting the earth aloft upon timber; they make a smoaky fire against the earth at the highest side, and thus these poor servants of Christ provide shelter for themselves, their wives and little ones, keeping off the short showers from their lodgings, but the long rains penetrate through, to their grate disturbance in the night season; yet in these poor wigwams, they sing Psalms, pray and praise their God, till they provide them homes, which ordinarily was not wont to be with many till the Earth, by the Lord's blessing brought forth bread to feed them, their wives and little ones."

Each house lot was "paled in" with sharpened sticks driven into the ground, and even this primitive dwelling generally had a garden about it. The "Assistants" of the Company sent by the first ships, seeds or cuttings of plum, filbert, cherry, pear, apple, quince, pomegranate and hop roots, and Johnson adds: "Let no man make a jest at pumpkins for with this fruit the Lord was pleased to feed his people to their good content till corne and cattell were increased."

Once established, the food was simple but nourishing. The meals centered on a thick soup of salt meat and pork thickened with pea and bean meal and to this was added hasty pudding and milk often both morning and evening. Later a more varied and generous fare was provided as indicated by the huge receptacles which have been left to us.

Our forefathers dined off wooden plates and pewter dishes and ate with spoons and curved knives. The luxury of a fork was not known until 1700. There was neither tea nor coffee to drink but plenty of home-brewed beer and cider and sometimes spirits.

The soil was good in the early days in spite of the rocks. Fish were plentiful and made excellent food as well as fertilizer for the fields. Corn was the principal staple. Rye also was common but wheat was sparingly planted. Pumpkins, melons, beans, peas and turnips also were in common use. Potatoes were not known in this locality for a hundred years after the founding of the colony. There were hay and oats for the cattle; flax for the fine linen woven on the hand looms and barley for beer. The scythe, the hoe and the hand rake were the chief implements.

The houses which followed the temporary huts were very simple affairs, some of them roofed with thatch. There was no sawmill until 1649. Previous to that, sawing was done in a saw pit by hand, one man below and one above. Every nail, hinge and bolt was forged by the village blacksmith. The houses were not expensive even for that day. Up to 1650, the cost of a house ranged from five pounds to thirty-six pounds. It was a rich man whose estate ran over one hundred pounds. This fact emphasizes the high value placed upon the John Whipple house already described. The

erection of buildings of a permanent character in the first
twenty years of any of the colonies was exceptional and
Ipswich has but two in existence which can claim, in any part
of their structure, to antedate 1650. It has preserved, however, many of those built during the last half of the XVIIth
and the early XVIIIth century. With its North Common
and South Common surrounded by these old mansions and
shaded by their magnificent elms it shares with its neighbors
Rowley and Newbury in retaining the flavor of the ancient
time, the mark of graceful age, which has not yielded to the
vulgarities of commercialism.

In this it has good precedent since, as has already been
suggested, it was in its beginnings essentially an aristocratic
community.

Class distinctions were quite as marked in early New England as in old England, though on a different basis. The men
whose names are mentioned above were distinguished and
granted special privileges because of the office they held in
the colony and not because of the social rank which they
brought with them. John Whipple was equally honored
although his station was that of a yeoman. In other words,
the church-state idea created a ruling class composed of the
minister, the elders, the selectmen and the representatives,
but eligibility to this class rested on orthodoxy rather than on
family. Marked distinction existed, however, between rich
and poor, learned and unlearned. We have already noted the
possession of worldly goods as evidenced by the more substantial dwellings of the well to do. One of the more elegant
houses of a later date than the Whipple house, marked by the
additions of many generations, is the Colonel Samuel Appleton homestead on South Main Street near the old stone bridge.

The original house is the south end (right hand) with its entrance on the south side facing a road which at that time passed in front of it. The house then fronted south instead of west as it does now. It was built by Shoreborn Wilson in 1682–92, and after several transfers was sold in 1702 to Colonel Samuel Appleton. The first Samuel Appleton established this well-known family in Ipswich within the first two years of its foundation. This descendant was the oldest son of Major Samuel Appleton who served in the expedition against Quebec in 1690 and again in 1706 as commissioner for the colonies to bring back prisoners. He returned with the Rev. John Williams of Deerfield, "The Redeemed Captive," and fifty-seven others. The house later on came into the hands of the Baker family with whom it has remained up to the present day.

The town-seal of Ipswich bears the legend, "The birthplace of American Independence, 1687." At its town meeting in that year its citizens rose up against Andros and refused to submit to taxation without representation. It was the pastor John Wise who planned this meeting and justified it in his "Vindication of the Government of the New England Churches" of which we have already spoken, and it was at the house of Samuel Appleton, though not the house we are discussing, that plans were laid the night before the meeting. The next day both Appleton and Wise were arrested.

To the original house has been added, by later generations, the north portion, and the entrance has been changed to face the present South Main Street. To these additions a lean-to was joined and last of all the Beverly ell at the north end. There are now four chimneys with fireplaces in every room.

The Colonel Samuel Appleton House. Ipswich, Mass.

The original door and entry remain on the south end but the stairway has been transferred to the present entrance. The south end has a low cellar and low studding while the newer end has a higher cellar and higher studding, with the result that no two rooms are on the same level, and the visitor experiences the delightful sensation of turning over a new page of history as he clambers in and out of each room, each stamped with the background of its own generation. The different levels are apparent in the location of the old windows as compared with the newer portion. In the old part also (right hand of illustration) to equalize the height of the first floor with those of the second floor, a strip of the house wall has been painted black to give the effect of a larger opening. The magnificent elm in the yard is one of the finest in the town which is proud of many beautiful trees.

There were evidences of wealth and position other than that of houses. We learn that Madame Symonds, wife of the Deputy Governor, followed the London fashions. There is abundant testimony to the fact that the clothing of the ladies and gentlemen of this primitive community was generally elegant and sometimes gay. The Rev. Nathaniel Rogers, who was pastor of Ipswich from 1638-55, was the wealthiest and most luxurious of the colonists. It was not long, however, before the General Court took note of this as it did of every other detail of the daily life of its citizens whose very consciences it assumed to control. In 1639 it launched a decree against extravagance in dress: "That no woman's sleeves shall be more than half an ell in width," and many other limitations. In general, that no person whose visible estate did not exceed two hundred pounds should wear buttons of gold or silver lace on penalty of ten

shillings for each offense.   Many men were fined for the
overdressing of their wives.   It was intended that all should
wear homespun and the Court ordained that children and
servants as well as adults should be employed in spinning
and weaving that the need for cloth might be met.   Ex-
travagances in attire were not confined to women, and men
were enjoined against long hair and instructed to crop their
locks short like the Round Heads.

An indulgence which came in for much attention from
the fathers was the use of tobacco.   The law read that:
"No person shall take tobacco publicly, in fine of 2/6 or
privately in his own home or another's house before ac-
quaintance or strangers."   Buying or selling tobacco was
prohibited in 1635.   In spite of this Pastor Rogers was an
inveterate smoker and his people persisted in cultivating
the weed.

As to strong drink, one individual only was licensed to
sell liquor in each town.   No man could remain in the ale-
house during the week day lecture.   As to Sunday, the laws
were many and penalties for infraction severe.   Sabbath
began Saturday at 3 P. M.   From that hour, time must
be spent in studying the catechism and preparing for Sunday in such manner as the teacher might direct; and there
were long hours in meeting, at least two sessions each Sunday.   No heat was furnished except from the foot stoves
which the good wives carried, nor were there pews with
backs; benches only in the early days.   It was not until
1675 that the first pew was permitted to Francis Wainwright.
The wall then became fashionable as against the center.
The old Ship Meeting House at Hingham, Mass., a replica
of which is now installed in the American wing of the Met-

ropolitan Museum, gives one the clearest impression of church going as our fathers endured it.

Men were fined for not knowing their catechism and for absence from meeting. In fact, no house could be built more than one half mile away from the meeting house. Penalties were inflicted for falling asleep during lecture. Indulgence in the last mentioned became so prevalent that one man was appointed for each congregation to keep its members awake with a long pole garnished with a fox tail, in some cases with a thorn.

The growing boys on the rear benches to which they were relegated, away from the control of their families caused much trouble during the lecture. It is told, for example, that one "Thomas Knowlton Jr. made a bad matter worse by calling out on the Lord's Day in prayer time, 'Take notice of Goodwife Hunt that makes disturbance there.'" For this Knowlton was sentenced to stand in the meeting house on the next lecture day during the entire reading, with a paper on his breast on which was written: "For disturbing ye meeting" and to "pay costs and fees."

The ministers generally managed to have the best houses. The Cobbet-Norton-Perkins house was built on the tract of land allotted to the Rev. John Norton, the third teacher of the First Church of Ipswich. A house adjoining was built by Thomas Firmin and sold to Mr. Norton in 1638 and he occupied it until he removed to Boston when he sold it to his successor, the Rev. Thomas Cobbet, who in turn sold it to Captain Matthew Perkins. Matthew Perkins was a weaver. His grandfather came to Ipswich in 1639 as the first of a long line of John Perkins of whom the ninth generation still lives in the town. The house

illustrated was built by Perkins about 1709, the original
Norton-Cobbet house adjoining, having been destroyed in
1818.

The spot is of interest as that whereon Norton lived and
wrote his works and where Mr. Cobbet gathered his neighbors

The Cobbet-Norton-Perkins House.   Ipswich, Mass.

to pray with him for his son who had been captured by the
Indians.   Here also Mugg, the Indian chief, stopped to visit
the pastor on his way to confer with the governor in Boston.

The house has an excellent double overhang and lean-
to.   The chimney has been restored, but on the ancient lines.
The interior has been much altered by many partitions and
is now occupied by two families.

Many of the Ipswich pastors became influential in the counsels of Massachusetts Bay. Perhaps its most eminent was its first, the Rev. Nathaniel Ward, known as the author of the code of law adopted by the General Court in 1641 and called "The Body of Liberties." Like many another of the early parsons who had been excommunicated by Archbishop Laud, he was against toleration. In his "Simple Cobbler of Agawam," he thus expresses it: "I dare take upon me to be the Herauld of New England so farre, as to proclaim to the world in the name of our Colony that all Familists, Anti-nomians, Anabaptists and other Enthusiasts shall have free liberty to keep away from us, and such as will come, to be gone as fast as they can, the sooner the better." [1]

The Emerson House on the Turkey Shore Road, is a good example of many of the XVIIth century houses of this locality and is one of the earliest. Thomas Emerson came to Ipswich in 1638 and bought six acres of land on this lane. Here he built this house in 1648 and sold it to Daniel Ringe. The road was, in the early days, merely a cart path known as Wood's Lane which led to the "Labor-in-Vain fields," so called because they lay opposite a bend in the river through which the ebb tide ran so swiftly that it was well nigh impossible to row a boat against it.

The house, though modernized to some extent, retains much of its original construction. Its shallow entry holds the stairway against the chimney which, in this case, is without handrail. Summers are in evidence in both parlor and hall as well as the corner posts. Where the rear fire-

---

[1] "American History Told by Contemporaries," edited by Albert Bushnell Hart, The Macmillan Company, 1902.

place was originally, the oven opening now only remains. The main front is the original building, the lean-to, as in most cases, having been added later.

Thomas Emerson's son was the Rev. John Emerson, for many years the minister at Gloucester. He was a class-

The Howard Emerson House.   Ipswich, Mass.

mate at Harvard of Robert Paine, son of the Elder Paine who gave the dwelling in Ipswich for the schoolmaster in 1650. In that year Ezekiel Cheever, the most eminent teacher in New England, was called to this school. Cotton Mather was one of his pupils and in his later years bore eloquent testimony to his qualities as a scholar and as a religious teacher. This grammar school prepared pupils

for Harvard. It is interesting to find the following requirements for entrance: "When scholars had so far profited at
the Grammar Schools that they could read any classical
author into English and readily make and speak true Latin
and write it in verse as well as prose; and perfectly decline

The Rigby House.   Ipswich, Mass.

the paradigms of nouns and verbs in the Greek tongue,
they were judged capable of admission to Harvard College."

The oblong two-and-a-half story, peaked-roofed, central-
chimney house now owned by Miss Rigby on North Main
Street is typical of many others of like age in the shore
settlements from Ipswich to Newburyport. Neither date
nor original builder are known. The probabilities favor

a date not later than 1725 and not earlier than 1700. It
has at different times been the home of several of Ipswich's
old families including the Heards, the Kimbals and Deacon Abraham Lord.

The "parlor," "hall" and entry have all the characteristic features of the primitive houses. The present owner
has painted the blinds orange and the front door black.
As the house is well shaded, this touch of bright color
against the white background strikes a note of gaiety which
is not inharmonious. The jog, so characteristic of later
additions, is this time attached to the rear rather than the
front as in the Judge Holten house.

A year after the founding of Ipswich, the Rev. Thomas
Parker arrived from England with about one hundred other
persons. The colony was becoming crowded about Boston
and the people of Cambridge had asked and had been granted
permission to find other locations. They considered Ipswich or vicinity first, but finally decided in favor of Connecticut as we know. Mr. Parker was called to Ipswich to
join the Pastor Nathaniel Ward but preferred to accompany
some of his countrymen from Wiltshire and with them sought
and established a new community further north. The name
Newbury was chosen in honor of Mr. Parker who came
from Newbury in England. Both Parker, and Noyes, who
went with him, were Presbyterians. The variation in belief was the cause of religious differences which divided the
community for many generations. Newbury sheltered also
several followers of Mrs. Anne Hutchinson, some of whom
were sent back to England for their erroneous religious
opinions. To these conflicting opinions were added those
of Whitfield who shortly arrived from England, the whole

resulting in that prolonged religious controversy which shook New England to its foundations.

One of Newbury's oldest and most characteristic homes is the Swett-Illsley house which, in its time, has been a primitive settler's dwelling, a family mansion and finally an

The Swett-Illsley House. Newbury, Mass.

ordinary or public tavern. It is now owned and maintained by the Society for the Preservation of New England Antiquities. The oldest part, the southern end (left hand of illustration), one room in width, was built by one Stephen Swett before 1670. This original house with its (then) chimney faced south instead of east as the house now fronts and its ridge ran at right angles to the ridge of the present house.

About 1700 it was enlarged by the present middle rooms, the present left entry added and the house made to face east towards the highway. The present main chimney was built at that time. The last addition was that at the northern end with its own entry, stairway and chimney.

The largest fireplace is in the middle room, nearly eleven feet opening and five feet in height. This room was at one time the barroom of the tavern. The rooms in the oldest part are sheathed with excellent paneling and show their original summers, girths and posts. The middle and southern portions only of the house have been restored.

The old house has had many owners between Stephen Swett and the Illsley family to whom it was deeded in 1797 and with whom it has remained until transferred to the Society for the Preservation of New England Antiquities, in 1911. One of its early owners, Captain John March, led a company in the attack on Canada in 1690 and commanded the attack on Damaris Cove, Maine, in 1697. He also defended the fort at Casco Bay against the French and their Indian allies so gallantly that he was rewarded by a grant of fifty pounds by the General Court. In 1773 it fell into the hands of Dudley Colman who served with Washington as lieutenant colonel on the Hudson River and at Valley Forge. Many times in its long life the old house has given hospitality to man and beast as a Post Road tavern between Boston and the frontier.

The Coffin House, still standing on High Street, was built about 1650 either by Tristram Coffin Jr. or by Henry Somersby, Mrs. Coffin's first husband. The original Tristram Coffin came from Brixton, Devonshire, settled first in Haverhill, moved from there to Salisbury, Mass. and in 1647 was granted the privilege by the General Court of keeping an ordinary in Newbury and of transferring passengers by ferry from that town to Salisbury. It was in 1660 that he moved with his family to Nantucket where he remained and where we hear of him in connection with the Jethro Coffin house.

The Coffin House. Newbury, Mass.

This house in Newbury represents the branch of the family which remained behind. Tristram Jr., the son, married in 1653, Judith Somersby, widow of Henry Somersby. She brought the house as her dowry, or Tristram built it at that time.

The present rear building is the original house which faced south and was built in the usual fashion about the single chimney. Tristram and Judith had ten children and it became necessary to have additional room. The addition across the east end was therefore built and the entrance changed to face the high road. Later the house was occupied by two families, the one using the south the other the east entrance. The porches are comparatively recent additions but with this exception the house is believed to be, in its exterior lines, substantially as it was when occupied by Tristram Jr. and his family. He was for twenty years deacon of the First Church of Newbury, a freeman of the colony and a representative of Newbury in the General Court. His descendants continuously occupied the homestead during the XVIIIth century and furnished several graduates of Harvard College. The most eminent descendant of the later generations was Joshua Coffin who came into possession of half the house in 1805. He was a graduate of Dartmouth and during the early years taught school in East Haverhill, Bradford, Mass., and Hampton, N. H. The poet Whittier was one of his pupils and has left a tribute to his character and achievements in which he speaks of him as:

> "Olden teacher, present friend,
> Wise with antiquarian search
> In the scrolls of State and Church
> Named on history's title page
> Parish clerk and justice sage."

It was in this house, where he was born and died, that he collected the material and prepared for publication the "History of Newbury." The house is said to contain many interesting relics. When photographed the windows and doors were boarded up and it appeared to be falling into decay.

This frontier participated in the Pequot War and that of King Philip and suffered, in a lesser degree than the coast of Maine, from the devastating inroads of French and Indians in the fighting of the XVIIIth century. A constant watch, day and night, was kept against the Tarantines and to this service, guests as well as residents were liable. A watch house was built near the Meeting House in Ipswich as late as 1745. Military training was the order of the day all along the coast. In fact, the danger of attack by the Indians, the chance of a rupture with the mother country, and the constant expectation of trouble with the French kept the outlying towns stirred up for many years.

The northern frontier of Massachusetts, however, while exposed, was in close touch with the General Court and its source of supply. The western frontier, on the other hand, was far removed from both and during the entire period of the French wars suffered from its isolation and scanty resources. At the outbreak of King Philip's War, Deerfield, originally Pocumtuck, was but just established on the Connecticut River. It consisted of 8000 acres allotted to Dedham to compensate that community for land at Natick dedicated by the Court to the uses of the Rev. John Eliot and his Indian mission. While the grant was made in 1663, it was not until 1669 that two pioneers, Samuel Hinsdale and Samson Frary, made the beginnings of this frontier post and it was ten years from the date of the grant before the General Court authorized these and other adventurers to organize a self-governing community, with the proviso that the new town should include a minister who should be orthodox, *i.e.*, acceptable to the court. The town street with numbered lots had been laid out in 1671 practically as it is now. Its nearest neighbor on the south was Hadley, fourteen miles away, itself a struggling outpost. To the north an unbroken wilderness stretched away to Canada; Albany was the nearest settlement on the west, while Lancaster and Brookfield were the nearest points east, at a distance of about fifty miles. Deerfield, therefore, when its history commences, was the northwestern frontier outpost of New England, a straggling hamlet of houses surrounded by a palisade with about a hundred and twenty-five inhabitants.

Samuel Mather, nephew of Eleazer Mather, who had been for ten years minister at Northampton was engaged as the first minister at an annual stipend of thirty-seven pounds. He was of the New Haven school of thought and thoroughly orthodox.

When Philip's braves took the warpath in 1675, Deerfield was attacked twice; first on September 1 and again on September 12 but managed to drive off the attackers with the aid of troops sent from Hadley to defend them. On the eighteenth Captain Lathrop was sent up to Deerfield with a troop to bring back to headquarters at Hadley the grain which was being harvested. Deerfield furnished the teamsters for the seventeen wagon loads. Two miles south, at the fording of a sluggish brook, the troop and convoy were ambushed by a large force of Indians, many of them recognized as Eliot's "praying Indians." The commander and a large part of his company fell at the first shot and not a single teamster returned to Deerfield to tell the tale. Captain Moseley came up from Hadley and held the Indians at bay for several hours although greatly outnumbered and Major Treat arrived finally in time to save the remnant. Sixty-three in all were slaughtered. The suddenness and the ferocity of the attack and the large proportion of those engaged who were killed profoundly affected the countryside and the Bloody Brook Massacre has been made the theme of many a song and story. All Deerfield literature is permeated with it and its recital forms the introduction to every family history. The town through which the stream still flows was named the village of Bloody Brook and so remained until, on petition of the Boston and Maine Railroad it was changed to South Deerfield. A monument marks the spot, and a stone near by the common grave of those that fell.

Bloody Brook was but the prelude to Deerfield's tragedies. Its immediate effect was the removal of the small garrison and the distribution of the few remaining families among the villages to the south. Sporadic attempts were made to re-build but even after the capture and death of Philip, maraud-ing bands of Indians infested the Connecticut valley ready to thwart efforts made to re-establish the outpost and effec-tually prevented it for several years. In 1682, however, permanent houses were rebuilt and the settlers began to re-turn to their farms with greater confidence in the future. A few years of peaceful development followed. Every disturb-ance of the relations, however, between France and England was immediately felt at this exposed frontier. The settlers themselves were not slow to recognize their danger and when border attacks by France's Indian allies followed the Revolu-tion of 1688, Deerfield proceeded to fortify its Meeting House hill with a palisade and to provide temporary quarters in case of attack within the fortification, for those compelled to live outside.

Every year now, during the next four or five, Deerfield was

subjected to attacks and between attacks was in daily fear of the return of the savages. The Peace of Ryswick brought a brief respite to be followed by still more ferocious reprisals for English and colonial victories elsewhere. It was in 1703 that French and Indians laid waste the coast of Maine after the declaration of war by Queen Anne. Deerfield awoke to its still greater danger and the Rev. John Williams, who now appears as the pastor of the struggling community, appealed to the General Court for protection and for remission of taxes during the war. "I lay it before your Excellency (the Governor) to move your compassion of us." He adds that he has abated his own salary and asks that rates be cancelled and the fort strengthened. The General Court actually voted Deerfield twenty pounds.

All this is preliminary to the greatest of village tragedies. On the last day of February, 1704 a force of French and Indians under Hertel de Rouville assaulted the palisaded town in the middle of the night. The French account reads: "They killed a large number and took a hundred and fifty prisoners." Inside the stockade were about fifteen houses, north of it twelve, and south fourteen. The part of the street south of the palisade was not raided and many houses at that end were not destroyed. Seventeen houses with their barns were burned and there were left standing nine within the enclosure and fifteen without. One house was held successfully by seven men against the horde and much damage inflicted on the enemy. The Rev. John Williams was attacked among the first and he, his wife and children were carried away as captives. The wife who was not able to maintain the pace of her captors was shortly tomahawked but the pastor, for two years captive in Canada, was brought back in 1706 with others by Major Appleton as previously noted. A year later he published the famous narrative of his experience under the name of "The Redeemed Captive."

The house of Ensign Sheldon, later known as the "Old Indian House" withstood the assault for some time by force of its own sturdy construction. Its heavy nail-studded oak door with its original posts is cherished in Memorial Hall as the most precious relic of Deerfield's most tragic episode. The hole cut through its two inch plank by the hatchet remains to make more real the tale so often told.

Forty-nine in all were slain on that memorable day and one hundred and eleven made captive. Some of the captives died from exposure or were slain on the journey, some of the girls married Indians and never returned, but the larger number was eventually ransomed and brought back.

A small body of troops from Hatfield attempted with the aid of those left in Deerfield to retake the prisoners but were overcome by superior numbers and nine of them were killed.

For the next fifty years fighting along the frontier was practically continuous and Deerfield was not entirely free from danger until the more energetic and capable Lord Geoffrey Amherst succeeded Abercrombie in command and successfully pushed the attack against the Canadian strongholds. Conditions in the Connecticut valley were, however, greatly improved by the construction and maintenance in 1744 of the cordon of forts which ran from Fort Dummer over the mountains to the New York line. These were merely picketed houses provided with mounts and at times of greatest danger garrisoned by colonial troops or militia in the pay of the colony, but were effective in holding off attacks from the villages themselves.

When the French power collapsed, the Indian ceased his activities and the last raid in 1759 marked his final exit from the stage of New England, but many generations will yet pass away before the bloody annals of his ferocity will be forgotten.

There is no more beautiful nor peaceful street in New England than the main street of old Deerfield. It is now the principal highway from New Haven north through Springfield to the White and Green mountains but the heavy traffic due to this fact has not disturbed the serenity of its two hundred and fifty years. The peaceful tenor of its life centers now, as of old, about the Meeting House hill near which the Deerfield Academy relieves what might otherwise be deemed its austerity by a touch of youth and gaiety. The magnificent elms which overarch the highway seem not less ancient than the houses which border it. The long lines of hills which lightly touch the sky encompass the smiling valley with a wall which removes it from a work-a-day world. All elements combine to form the harmonious whole which charms the traveler and inspires him with the hope of a speedy return to its peaceful shades.

The "Old Indian House," a mention of which has been made, though fired during the raid in 1704, was saved, and survived as the most interesting house of the early period until 1848 when unfortunately it was torn down and the door only and its posts saved. Two, at least, of the houses still standing antedate the catastrophe of 1704. Others bordering the long Main Street have been built since that time.

Directly opposite the spot where the Old Indian House stood is the Willard house, sometimes called the Manse because it became the residence of the Rev. Dr. Samuel Willard. The gambrel-roofed ell in the rear is the oldest building now standing in Deerfield. Robert Hinsdale, the first owner of the lot on which it stands, was killed with Captain Lathrop in the battle of Bloody Brook and his successor deeded the lot with a house on it, undoubtedly the small cottage in question, in 1694. It was built therefore, some time between the original grant in 1671 and the above date, and it escaped destruction in 1704. In the attack, however, Samuel Carter, the owner, and four of his children were made captive and taken to Canada, while his wife and the other children were killed. Carter was redeemed and returned with one of the children, the others remaining in Canada, two as wives of Indian chiefs. Samuel Allen, grandfather of Col. Ethan Allen next lived in the gambrel cottage and from him it passed to the Barnard family who in 1768 built the square, hip roof, two chimney Georgian house in front.

Dr. Willard came into possession of the property in 1807 and during his lifetime it was the center of the intellectual life of the community and opened its doors to the brilliant men of that period including Horace Greeley, Francis Parkman, Charles Sumner and Ralph Waldo Emerson. His ordination as minister marked the beginning of the Unitarian movement in western Massachusetts.

The wide overhang of the gambrel story is to be noted. The chimney occupies most of the center of the lower floor which has one room at the east end and a narrow chamber at the end adjoining the later addition. The stair rises between the chimney and chamber.

The main house is of very harmonious proportions. The

rooms are high with elaborate wainscoting of native pine
and heavy Georgian cornices and are floored with one-and-
a-quarter pine running from eight to fourteen inches wide.
The house faces directly west and has a doorway and broad
hall on each of the four sides.   The main stairway is elabo-

The Willard House.   Deerfield, Mass.

rate with a very fine hand-carved newel post.   The summers
are exposed in three of the first-floor rooms and are parallel
to the chimney girth and about twelve by fourteen in size.
In the "parlor" the timbers do not show and were presumably "buried" for greater elegance.   The fireplaces
are large and without mantels, while to conserve the warmth
the walls are filled with brick and plaster.   The most interesting room is that now used as a dining room on the

northeast corner, which has a very fine large brick fireplace with oven.

Three lots south of the Willard house on the same side
of the street stands the Samson Frary house which is next
in point of age. In the harmonious union of its two sections, built nearly a hundred years apart, and in its excellent state of preservation, it is one of the most interesting
of old New England homesteads.

Mr. Sheldon, the historian of Deerfield, tells us that
Samson Frary, son of John of Medfield was of Hatfield in
1668 and came to Deerfield, the second known settler, in
1670. He was killed in the sack of the village by Hertel de
Rouville in 1704. Frary is credited with having built the
north end (without the addition) in 1689 and this was one
of the houses, south of the palisade, which escaped destruction in this memorable catastrophe.

The south end was built by Salah Barnard in 1763 and
the whole used as a tavern. Like other taverns of the pre-
Revolutionary period it was a social and political center,
and though in the early days of the conflict Deerfield was
strongly Tory in sentiment, Mr. Sheldon gives us an interesting incident of its history, which connects it with the
first capture of Ticonderoga. A week after Deerfield had
responded to the call to arms by sending a contingent to
Cambridge, there arrived at the tavern a Continental officer who announced himself as Benedict Arnold and showed
his commission as colonel from the Provincial Assembly.
He stopped in the taproom and sent for Thomas Dickinson. To him he confided his plan which was by a sudden
dash to take the fort of Ticonderoga. By authority of the
Assembly he gave Dickinson a commission as assistant

commissary and directed him to furnish 15,000 lbs. of beef for the prospective army. This done he rode away. Dickinson promptly set out with fifteen steers but met the force returning from the north, after the capture. Arnold was in Deerfield on May 6 and while he was still organizing

The Samson Frary House.   Deerfield, Mass.

his force, Ticonderoga was taken by Ethan Allen and his Green Mountain boys.

The north end is the typical central chimney house with lean-to apparently built as part of the original building. The north room at the left of the entrance, has a fireplace, diminished in size from the original, set in excellent paneling of mid-eighteenth century type.   The summer is en-

The Samson Frary House. Deerfield, Mass. North End.

cased. The south room, the original "Hall" is also paneled, with reduced fireplace and summer. From this room the rear door leads to the lean-to, originally the kitchen, which has a very large brick fireplace. This room has been transformed into a very delightful morning room with French leaded windows opening on the garden, a necessary adjunct to every Deerfield home.

The shallow entry shows the usual stairway rising on the left and turning to the right with an opening facing the entrance which presumably led to the cellar stairway. Upstairs the parlor chamber has its summer encased, while the hall chamber has a chambered summer without paneling.

The outer walls are sided with the narrow clapboards of the earliest Massachusetts period nailed with anvil-wrought nails. The chimney is of brick from the first floor up.

The south addition has direct connection with the older building on both floors. On the ground floor the barroom in the southwest corner (front) has a large fireplace and a bar with a stair running to the cellar by which liquors were brought to the bar without passing through the public rooms. On the second floor is a ballroom of excellent proportions. The windows of the east end of the room are arched, suggesting its ceremonial character, while the opposite end is devoted to a graceful gallery for the musicians. Along the sides run settles with step raised above the level of the floor. These performed the double function of seats for the onlookers and receptacles for the outer garments of the guests, which were stowed under the hinged seats.

The old house has played a double rôle, that of a primitive homestead and of a pre-Revolutionary tavern and maintains admirably its character as typical of both.

In harmony with its surroundings and possessing its own ancient flavor it continues a residence of charm and distinction to the present day.

The "Little Brown House on the Albany Road" as Mr. Sheldon, historian of Deerfield, has named it, is interesting

The Little Brown House on the Albany Road.
Deerfield, Mass.

mainly for its picturesque line and surroundings and to show what practical adaptation to modern uses can be made of the old houses. Originally a single chimney, peaked roofed cottage of the Cape Cod type, it has been transformed into a studio by the addition of the dormer to the front slope of the roof.

Built about 1760, it was the house of David Saxton, shoemaker, who kept a tavern which became headquarters for the Whigs during the Revolution. The cottage's most distinguished resident was Epapheras Hoyt, author of "Antiquarian Researches."

The Beaman Allen House is a good example of the oblong two-and-a-half story house to which a later lean-to

The Beaman Allen House.   Deerfield, Mass.

addition has been made. The flatter angle of the lean-to than the original peaked roof is plainly shown in the illustration. On this lot stood in 1694 the first school house and Hannah Beaman was the school mistress. At the assault in 1704 she, her husband and a servant, were captured, carried to Canada, and later were ransomed and brought back. This house was occupied by them after their return and was presumably built before 1722. It has lost its chimney and the interior has been modernized but it retains its characteristic line and fits admirably into its surroundings.

The Bardwell-Stebbins-Abercrombie house faces the street from a slight eminence a little further north. It was built

The Bardwell-Stebbins-Abercrombie House. Deerfield, Mass.

in 1771 after the close of the French wars and was for many years used as a tavern. A square two and half story, one chimney house without lean-to but with a rear ell which appears of the same date, with separate chimney. In the main chimney are three fireplaces on the first floor and originally two on the second. The chimney is of great size and of brick throughout. Summers show in all three lower rooms. The south front room (window at left of illustration) was the barroom of the tavern. The east room (doorway) has a very fine large brick fireplace with oven. The main entry on the front is not as shallow as those of houses built before 1700. The stairway rises directly against the chimney for four steps to a landing; from the landing steps run to right and to left to the north and south chambers without intervening hallway. The north chamber ran originally the full length of the house and was used as a ballroom. The baluster and spindles of the stairway are square and plain. Its proportions are, however, exceptionally pleasing.

The Rev. John Williams house was built by the town for the pastor after his return from captivity in 1707. The original house was built also for him on the same lot in 1686 but was destroyed in the attack of 1704. Two children and a servant were murdered at the first onset, but the wife, the pastor and the other children were captured alive, as already mentioned. Of the children one, Eunice, remained in Canada, married an Indian and lived to a ripe old age.

The present house which has been moved west a few hundred feet from its original location was in 1789 sold by Mr. Williams' grandson to Consider Dickinson whose widow left it and the rest of her estate to the town as a foundation for a free academy and Public Library. The present Deerfield Academy, whose dormitories and lecture rooms surround the old house, is the outcome of the bequest and has recently restored the house itself.

Originally a single-chimney, lean-to house it was extensively altered in 1756 and the main chimney was removed to allow for the central hallway of a Georgian house. Two smaller chimneys were substituted providing for fireplaces

The John Williams House. Deerfield, Mass.

· in both front and back rooms. The interior is now finished in excellent paneling throughout. Summers and posts remain but are paneled.

"The Redeemed Captive," in his narrative of which the subtitle is "Returning to Zion," includes a poem indited in Quebec in which he epitomizes the sufferings of those with him, and his own. "Sorrowful, mournful considerations" which "though unused and unskilful in poetry, yet in a plain style . . . are here made publick."[1]

"Contemplations of the poor and desolate state of the church at Deerfield:

> "The sorrows of my heart enlarged are,
> Whilst I my present state with past compare
> I frequently unto God's house did go,
> With Christian friends his praises forth to show.
> But now I solitary sit, both sigh and cry,
> Whilst my flock's misery think on do I.
> Many, both old and young were slain outright,
> Some in a bitter season took their flight,
> Some burnt to death and others stifled were:
> The enemy no sex or age would spare.
> The tender children, with their parents sad,
> Are carried forth as captives some unclad,
> Some murdered in the way, unburied left,
> And some through famine were of life bereft.
> After a tedious journey, some are sold
> Some kept in heathen hands, all from Christ's fold
> By popish rage and heathenish cruelty
> Are banished. Yea some compelled to be
> Present at Mass. Young children parted are
> From parents, and such as instructors were
> Crafty designs are used by papists all,
> In ignorance of truth, them to enthrall.
> Some threatened are, unless they will comply

[1] "The Redeemed Captive," by Rev. John Williams, Northampton, Hopkins Bridgman & Co., 1853.

In heathen's hands again be made to lie.
To some, large promises are made, if they
Will truths renounce and choose their popish way.
Oh Lord! Mine eyes on thee shall waiting be,
Till thou again turn our captivity."

This was after some eight months of captivity in October, 1704, and it was not until November 21, 1706, that Williams and fifty-seven others, including two of his children, were finally landed in Boston. This happy outcome of all his sufferings prompts him to conclude:

"At our arrival in Boston, we found the kindnesses of the Lord in a wonderful manner, in God's opening the hearts of many, to bless God with us and for us, wonderfully to give for our supplies in our needy state. We are under obligations to praise God, for disposing the hearts of so many to so great charity, and under great bonds to pray for a blessing on the heads, hearts and families of them, who so liberally and plentifully gave for our relief."

And forthwith he delivered himself of his Sermon, preached at Boston, December 5, 1706, on the text from Luke 8: 39 "return to thine own house, and shew how great things God hath done unto thee."

CHAPTER V

INTOLERANCE AND EXPANSION

◇◆◇◆◇◆◇OGER Williams, graduated at twenty-three from Cambridge, was thrown, in the work of his chaplaincy, with the many Anabaptists and Mennomites who were at that time emigrating from Cambridgeshire to New England. He accepted such fundamentals from them as the separation of Church and State, the principle that the magistrate shall punish offenses against man but that sin against God shall be left to the judgment of the individual conscience. In Boston, which he reached five years later, he found an ecclesiastical oligarchy enforcing a religious discipline not at all in accord with his views of the freedom of the individual conscience. To these heresies, in the view of Endicott and his ministers, he added the conviction that the Massachusetts colonists held their land directly from the King and not through purchase from the Indians under their charter. The colony was even then preparing to maintain its position on this question against Charles by force if necessary and the outspoken criticism of the young Salem pastor was peculiarly offensive. After Salem he tried Plymouth, but found there the same unyielding rigidity and so returned to Salem. It was in October, 1635, four years after his arrival, that he was ordered to depart within six weeks. The time of his leaving was extended until spring but discovering that he continued proselytizing, it was determined to send him back to England in January. To John Underhill was allotted the task of arresting him. Warned in time, Williams escaped through the forest in midwinter, to the lodge of Massasoit, Sachem of the Wampanoags, whose friendship he had gained during his sojourn in Plymouth. That the Indian chiefs knew and respected him and that he had acquired a knowledge of the Algonquin tongue were facts of signal value in the founding and maintenance of the new colony. To do something for the Indians was one of the main purposes which had brought him to New England. To this was now added another which became the moving and vital motive of his life; to establish a refuge for those who, like himself, fleeing the intolerance and persecution at home, could not accept the rigid theocracy of Massachusetts and Plymouth.

In founding his community he followed the advice of his friend, Governor Winthrop, who privately suggested to him that he choose Narragansett as his location. He built a house at Seekonk, on the east side of the river of that name, now East Providence, but was advised by his friend Governor Winslow that there he was in territory claimed by Plymouth. Winslow added that if he would retire to the west side of the river he would see to it that he should not be molested. This advice also he followed and called the spot "Providence," since in respect to "freedome and vacancie, it was one of many Providences of the most Holy and only Wise."

The year following the settlement, the Pequot War broke out with all its fury and Williams with no thought of the treatment under which he had suffered, freely gave his share of service to the whole land.

In a letter written in 1670, thirty-five years after his

establishment, he himself expresses what he believes to have been his service: [1]

"The matter with us is not about these children's toys of land, meadows, cattell, government etc. But here, all over this colonie a great number of weak and distressed soules, scattered, are flying hither from Old and New England, the most High and only Wise hath, in his infinite wisdom provided this country and this corner as a shelter for the poor and persecuted, according to their several persuasions. . . .

"This, sir, the King's majestie hath vouchsafed his royall promise that no person in this colony shall be molested or questioned for the matters of his conscience to God . . . Sir, we must part with lands and lives before we part with such a jewall."

No part of Rhode Island was settled by organized churches as were the other colonies. "Weake and distressed soules" to use Williams' phrase, dissatisfied with the established order and driven from one colony to the other, here found peace. Coddington and Clarke of the Antinomians (*i.e.*, those opposed to forms), following the trial of Mrs. Hutchinson and Wheelwright, obtained a grant of Aquidneck from Canonicus through Williams' intervention and founded Portsmouth. Mrs. Hutchinson came later and Coddington and Clarke retired further south and founded Newport. Always at odds with each other these two settlements finally joined forces and came under Providence Plantations. Then came Gorton, a familist and always an extremist and a thorn in the flesh to Roger Williams.

[1] "American History Told by Contemporaries," edited by Albert Bushnell Hart, The Macmillan Company, 1902.

Driven from Portsmouth and Pawtuxet, he at length established his claim to Shawomet.

Last to be established was the Narragansett country or King's Province, as it was called, which joined Connecticut. Connecticut's charter, obtained of the home government by John Winthrop, Jr., gave her territory to the "Narragansett River." A charter also had been given the Atherton Company, composed of many English noblemen, of whom Winthrop was one. Although the commissioners in 1665 placed this territory under the Rhode Island patent and cancelled the company's charter, the controversy over the conflicting claims did not subside until well into the XVIIIth century.

Settled by those who were against the established order; outcasts in the Puritan view; abhorred by Massachusetts, which sought on every occasion to obtain control of its territory; beset by Connecticut, not so much for religious reasons as from a strong desire for expansion eastward; the poorest of all the colonies, Rhode Island, survived. Its charter obtained with difficulty in 1663, though often in abeyance, held sway until the Revolution. Its great and signal accomplishment was the separation of church and state for the first time in history; the establishment of the rights of man as a being responsible to God and not to the community.

To the single mindedness and high purpose of Roger Williams alone may be credited these achievements. When he died in 1683 the four towns, Providence, Portsmouth, Warwick and Newport, had grown but little. In the early XVIIIth century commerce brought much prosperity however, which continued in increasing volume until after the

Revolution.   Commerce was followed by manufactures which have been the source of great wealth to the industrial centers but agriculture has never flourished and remains as backward today as at the time of the Revolution.

Williams was an Anabaptist as was Mrs. Hutchinson, and the Anabaptists became the dominant sect, to be followed by the Quakers.   Roger Williams built the first Baptist Meeting House on the side of the hill facing the present civic center of Providence, where now stands the present structure built in 1775, one of the most satisfying interpretations of the work of Sir Christopher Wren on this continent.   Nearby, toward the river, the first houses were built, that of Williams among them.   None of these remain; the Roger Mowry Tavern which was torn down in 1900 was the last of that period to survive.   We have already considered the James Greene house at Buttonwoods, one of the primitive houses of Providence Plantations (Chapter I) as well as that of Governor Bradford and John Brown representing later periods (Chapter II).

In 1639 Richard Smith built the first trading post in the Narragansett territory at Cocumscussic which is now Wickford.   A few years later Roger Williams himself went there to trade.   It is reported that to raise money for his voyage to England to obtain the charter, Williams sold Smith land and houses at this point and two cannon for his protection. The first building was a garrison house as well as a trading post and served as headquarters for the colonial troops during the campaign which ended in the swamp fight.   On the edge of the swamp a few rods in front of the house is a tablet which marks the grave of forty men who fell in this fight.   After their defeat in the swamp, the Indians burned the trading houses. The present building was constructed of material taken from the older house by Richard Smith the younger in 1680.

Here we have a central chimney house of the Newport type. There are two large square front rooms with a stair-

The Richard Smith Block House. Wickford, R. I.

way between, leading to the second story and also to the cellar. The stairs rise against the chimney but the entry is somewhat wider and deeper than usual. Each front room has a large fireplace with crossed summers, the beam running at right angles to the chimney carrying the load of the floor above. This is an unusual construction. These summers are now encased and there is some good paneling in the dining room.   Back of the mid line of the house there are three smaller rooms and a hall.   The middle one of these rooms has a fireplace running to the main chimney, the other rooms have none and are doubtless later additions.

The "Brown Bread Place."   East Greenwich, R. I.

The foundation of the chimney is very large and is of stone. The piazzas are, of course, a modern addition.

In East Greenwich, adjoining the Winston Spencer place is a typical house of the South County which follows the Newport and Connecticut tradition.   It is known as the "Brown Bread Place" and was, in all probability, built in the first few years of the XVIIIth century.   The west or left-hand end is the older portion, the small ell being a re-

cent addition. It is a single-chimney house with three fireplaces on each floor, shallow entry and narrow stairs. The
east end of the house is three stories in height, made possible
by a drop in the land on that side, and provides a lower

Mowbra Castle. Wickford, R. I.

story which has the largest of the fireplaces. The chimney
therefore carries flues for seven fireplaces in all.

Another house well known throughout the King's Province is the old Phillips' house of Wickford popularly known
as "Mowbra Castle." It was built between 1695–1700 by
Michael Phillips who came here from Newport. The older
part, shown at the right end of the illustration, consists of
the present ell and a part of the present main building. The

chief architectural feature of the exterior is the fine stone pilastered chimney. The foundation is very large and nearly square. The old rooms in the ell have some very fine paneling.

The stone chimney is peculiarly symbolic of the New England home. Found in the north but more frequently in the south country where suitable stone is abundant, they sometimes have pilasters with fine lines, as this one shows; sometimes they are square but always solid and substantial. The big chimney with its correspondingly huge fireplace and its suggestion of a sizzling roast turning on the spit and the oven filled with good things, expresses the material plenty, the essential home atmosphere with the patriarch and his numerous children and grandchildren gathered about the ancestral fireside.

Of the native New England tribes the Pequots were the most warlike and aggressive. Their continued assaults on the planters made the new settlements on the Connecticut River difficult and precarious and brought the colonists to the determination that a decisive blow must be struck to establish the superiority of the white man in the territory occupied. In this undertaking Connecticut had the support of Massachusetts. In addition, the aid of the Mohegan tribe of eastern Connecticut, led by their astute Sachem, Uncas, was assured. An alliance with the Narragansetts, the most numerous of the New England tribes, was also arranged through the intervention of Roger Williams, though in the final conflict the latter were merely spectators. Up to this time the Pequots had been considered invincible and doubt of the ability of the settlers to overcome them was freely expressed by their Indian allies.

The Pequot country lay directly west of the King's Province, of which we have been speaking, and extended from the east bank of the Connecticut to the present Rhode Island border and as far north as Norwich. The stronghold of the Pequots, a stockade in which were gathered the wigwams of the warriors, their squaws and their offspring, was located on a rise of land since known as Pequot Hill just north of Groton and about six miles from New London. The little army of the attackers included less than a hundred Massachusetts and Connecticut men and some two hundred Mohegans with a contingent of Narragansetts well in the rear. Captain John Mason of Windsor on one side and Captain John Underhill of Massachusetts on the other led the assault, which was so overwhelmingly successful that the Pequot tribe, as such, ceased thereafter to exist.

The land and the river, however, so intimately associated in the minds of the colonists with their warlike foes continued for many years to bear the name Pequot, and it was not until the territory became formally and legally a part of Connecticut that English names were substituted.

Massachusetts made claim to the tract as having participated in its capture, and granted to John Winthrop, Jr., Fisher's Island at the mouth of the Pequot River. Connecticut confirmed this grant. He had a stone house built on the main land for his family, from the quarry now known as Quaker Hill. The original type of house appears to have been a one or two room dwelling to which a lean-to was added. Many of the oldest houses were destroyed in the sack of New London under Benedict Arnold in 1781 and but few evidences of the founding in 1647 remain. The New England commissioners, somewhat later, decided against Massachusetts and the jurisdiction of the Pequot territory was given to Connecticut whose General Court, with characteristic diplomacy, appointed John Winthrop, Jr., as its representative and authorized him to administer Connecticut laws in the territory. In 1658 the Connecti-

The Hemstead House.   New London, Conn.

cut Assembly named the new settlement, "New London" and the river, "Thames," considering: "that we might therefore leave to posterity memory of that renowned city of London from whence we had our transportation."

The oldest of New London houses is the homestead of the Hemstead family. The older portion, the corner shown in the illustration, was built by Robert Hemstead, one of the original settlers in 1647. The eastern end, to the right of the chimney was built by this man's son in 1678 as indicated in the Hemstead diary. During King Philip's War, the original building was used as a block house, its solid construction warranting such use, and in the attack on New London in 1781 it was one of the few houses which escaped. The original was an end-chimney house, though probably the chimney was not exposed. In its construction it is the usual solid affair, stone to the third floor and brick above.

The main room in the older part shows the sills above the floor and a very large summer supported by a heavy post at each end. This timber runs parallel to the chimney and is repeated on the second floor. The room on the east end, of later date, has two summers at right angles to the chimney. The entry is shallow, with a door to the cellar, excavated under the old part only, and the stair to the second story on the left.

The homestead is now the property of the Hemstead Family Association which holds its reunions here annually and has been continuously the home of the ten generations of this stock since 1647.

The old Huguenot house on the corner nearby, was built for the fifth generation of the Hemstead family in 1751 by Huguenot refugees. It is also called the "Stone House" from the fact that its entire construction is of stone. Its two chimneys are built into the end walls with fireplaces in each room.

From the beginning, Dorchester, Watertown and Newtown, settlements about Boston, were opposed to the theocracy of the other five towns of Massachusetts Bay and refused to limit voters to church members. Hooker, Stone and

Haynes were at Newtown, the two first mentioned graduates
of Emmanuel College, Cambridge.   Hooker with a very clear
conception of democratic doctrine was silenced by the General Court for non-conformity in 1629 and was compelled
to support himself by teaching school.   His assistant at

The Huguenot House.   New London, Conn.

this time was John Eliot, later the apostle to the Indians.
A year later he returned to Holland and again took up
preaching and, after two years in this field, he was enabled
to return to Newtown with authority, as the Pastor of the
Community.   Stone was at the same time made teacher.

The three towns were granted permission to move in
1634, by the General Court which suggested the Merrimack

country but objected to the Connecticut valley. The towns gave as their reasons for choosing the latter, the lack of room where they were, the desire to save the Connecticut valley from the Dutch and "the strong bent of their spirits to move thither." John Cotton preached against it and the project was in abeyance for another year but the "strong bent of their spirits" prevailed and Massachusetts was induced to loan the communites' cannon and ammunition in 1635 to make a beginning in the valley. In this year also John Winthrop, Jr., was sent to Saybrooke as "Governor of the Connecticut River." The rigorous winter of 1635-36 was a hard one for the first arrivals but in the spring Hooker and Stone led the pilgrims through the forest with their cattle and all their worldly goods. Dorchester settled Windsor with Mr. Warham as their pastor, Newtown settled Hartford (named from Hertford, England, Stone's birthplace) with Hooker as pastor and Watertown settled Weathersfield without a pastor. John Talcot (spelled Tailcoat in the original record), from Weathersfield, England, was one of the leaders of the Watertown company.

The three towns began as organized churches as well as towns. Until 1727 the same body decided religious as well as political questions. It was then divided into the "Church and the Society," the Society representing the town meeting. At no time did Connecticut require church membership of voters. Those not satisfied with this more liberal government betook themselves to New Haven where rigidity and aristocracy walked hand in hand.

In the Connecticut valley the independence of the town was a political factor of great importance, since the colony came to be governed by a federation of these towns and their representatives constituted the governing body in which the power of taxation and other administrative functions rested. The federal principle adopted for the constitution of the United States in 1787 was patterned after the primitive union of these three towns. This union was embodied in the first written constitution known to history and was adopted by a popular convention of the three towns about two years after their arrival.

For several years after, the settlers were concerned with questions of territory and jurisdiction. With Massachusetts, Rhode Island, and even with their immediate neighbors of New Haven, the legal status of the new colony was constantly in question. Established under a permit from the Plymouth Company through Lord Say and Seale and Lord Brooke, grantees, it became necessary to establish their claim with the home government to their own locations; with the above grantees to the Saybrooke section who had appointed John Winthrop, Jr. their representative in Boston and George Fenwick at the mouth of the Connecticut River; with Massachusetts to the Pequot territory and with the Atherton Company and Roger Williams to their eastern boundary.

These negotiations were managed with astuteness and a wise diplomacy which brought a successful issue to their projects. The crowning achievement of this effort, sustained for more than twenty years, was the charter granted to John Winthrop, Jr., in 1662, by Charles II, of which we have already spoken. The address to the king was the result of the combined labors of the best intellect of the colony. Addressing the monarch in the flamboyant style of the period petition was made that a patent be granted on the basis of that formerly granted Lord Say and Seale and Lord Brooke or that of Massachusetts. In the final result the charter granted such full autonomy to the colony that no occasion arose to change it until the adoption of the state constitution in 1818. Incidentally it brought to an end the struggle of New Haven for separate existence and the perpetuation of the theocracy in the southern colony.

The first houses of the leaders of the migration were built along the north bank of the little river which flows into the Connecticut at Hartford. The dwellings of Governor Haynes, Mr. Hooker, Mr. Stone and Elder Goodwin were built in a line facing the road which ran along the bank of the stream aforesaid. The lane separating the houses of Hooker and Stone was called "Meeting House Alley." None of these, nor contemporary, buildings remains and in Connecticut as in the other colonies we must seek the oldest vestiges of the early settlement outside the industrial centers.

At Windsor, a few miles north of the Dutch Post called "Fort Good Hope," the Dorchester emigrants found a small settlement already established. The beginning had been made by William Holmes, from Plymouth, in 1633, the same year that John Winthrop, Jr. founded Ipswich. The original town of Windsor was located on the small stream which is now called the Farmington River. It consisted of a number of houses built, as was the custom, about the green with the Meeting House in the center. At the outbreak of the Pequot War the townspeople at once proceeded to prepare themselves for a possible attack. The fortifications erected consisted of a high palisade supplemented by a ditch, surrounding the entire group of houses.

The plan of this "Palizado" as it was called, still exists and has been reproduced in Mr. J. H. Hayden's "History of Hartford County." The green with the palisade coincides with the present green which now includes one of the oldest of Congregational churches which was built before 1650, on a plot granted to a settler named Gibbs.

The Palisade enclosed twenty-two homestead plots with the Meeting House and included the burying ground in one corner. Guard was kept for some time but Windsor was never attacked.

In 1640, three years after the destruction of the Pequots, Sergeant, later Lieutenant, Walter Fyler was granted one and one half acres in the Palisade for a home, in recognition of his services in the war, and built thereon a house. The cottage facing the green from the south end, its garden running to the rivulet, is a combination gable and gambrel roof, the gambrel section partaking of the Dutch colonial type. Additions have been made by subsequent owners and the interior divided into various small chambers to suit the taste of its many tenants. The records show that the original house included a parlor, parlor chamber, hall and hall chamber with a lean-to, so that it was beyond question originally a typical Connecticut two story, central chimney house with peak roof continued in a lean-to. The gambrel ell was a later addition built in 1794 with the present chimney, which serves two fireplaces in the gambrel, substituted for the original chimney stack in the gable roof. There are two interesting portraits in the parlor. One of Captain Stephen Fyler who was born here in 1755 and one of his wife Polly Collier Fyler. Their marriage was celebrated in this house.

The Fyler House. Windsor, Conn.

The property is now owned by the Windsor Historical Society and is maintained as a meeting place for the descendants of the Windsor families.

In the Older Williams house of Wethersfield, built about 1680, we have the typical two story, central chimney gable roof house without the lean-to. This is an excellent example

The Older Williams House.   Wethersfield, Conn.

of the second period in the development of the Connecticut houses and resembles the Parson Capen house of Topsfield, Mass., without its overhangs and decorations. The chimney occupies its usual location, with fireplaces on both floors and stairs to the cellar as well as to the second floor in front of the entrance.

In the Talcott-Arnold house of Rocky Hill the rectangular gable roof, central chimney, two story house has been expanded by the addition of the lean-to at a flatter angle than the original roof. The large chimney is here of brick as is generally the case in Connecticut outside of Guilford where gneiss was plentiful.

The Talcott-Arnold House. Rocky Hill, Conn.

The Whitman house of Farmington built about 1660 is the only XVIIth century house left in that town which a few years ago had preserved at least three of the oldest houses of the Connecticut valley. This old mansion is in an excellent state of preservation and although the clapboards have been removed and more modern windows have replaced the original leaded panes, it retains most of its original features. The rear ell is a modern addition.

The house in its general plan resembles the John Whipple house of Ipswich described in Chapter II and other XVIIth

The Whitman House. Farmington, Conn.

century houses. The chimney is built of flat field stone below the roof, laid in clay mixed with hay; above the roof it is of red sandstone. The front overhang is unusually good, measuring twenty inches in width, while the touch of distinction necessary for a parson's dwelling is contributed by the four hewn drops.

The interior also follows the traditions of the period, with summers, posts and girths exposed. In the hall, which is somewhat longer than the parlor, the walls are wainscoted with wide boards nailed on horizontally instead of perpendicularly as in the Whipple house. The summers run at right angles to the chimney. The lean-to is of later

The Banning House. Wethersfield, Conn.

construction than the main house and has a fireplace built against the old chimney.

This house was sold in 1735 to the Rev. Samuel Whitman who was engaged as Farmington's minister, for his son Solomon. He was a Harvard graduate of the class of 1696. His granddaughter, Ann Sophia, married in 1839, Henry Farnam. Mr. Farnam was an engineer much interested in railroads and was consulting engineer for the

Farmington Canal. His name is a household word among Yale men since he donated $60,000 for Farnam Hall which is still in use at New Haven as a dormitory.

The Banning house of Wethersfield, built in 1775, with its gambrel roof and double overhang is typical of Revolutionary building in Connecticut where the gambrel was adopted somewhat later than in Massachusetts.

In this house the central chimney and the shallow entry persist although in other colonies by this date the chimneys had been moved to the ends of the house and the central hallway of Georgian origin substituted for the steep stair against the chimney. This house in its conservative simplicity retains many of the features of the earlier homesteads rather than those of its contemporaries. The railing of its steep stair is without spindles, for example, while the framing, summers and posts are exposed and without paneling. In its retention of these early characteristics it is in contrast to the Webb house of Wethersfield built a little earlier and similar in general plan, but with many of the Georgian characteristics of the contemporary houses in the other colonies.

The Noah Webster house of West Hartford is notable, mainly for its connection with the great lexicographer. Its harmonious simplicity, however, again reminds us of the conservatism of the community of which it and he were a part.

Noah Webster was born in this house in 1758 and it is understood that the house was then about seventy-five years old. This places the date of the original construction at about 1683. The rear ell and the porch are later additions. Although the main part of the building is of wood, the rear wall is brick. At present the house is painted a dark red with white trimmings, a very harmonious effect in its background of trees and shrubbery.

Noah Webster was descended from John Webster, an early Governor of Connecticut, on his father's side and from Wil-

The Noah Webster House. West Hartford, Conn.

liam Bradford, the second Governor of Plymouth, on his mother's side, and came therefore of unadulterated Puritan stock. His own life began during the sufferings and bloodshed of the French and Indian War. By means of many sacrifices he was enabled to enter as a student at Yale but his course was interrupted by the War for Independence and the events preceding it. He succeeded, however, in graduating at twenty. The years which followed were the most difficult of his life. His father gave him eight dollars in continental currency, when he graduated, and told him to shift for himself. He managed by teaching to earn enough money to complete his law course and to gain admittance to the Bar. This was in 1781. Finding the practice of law unprofitable he resumed teaching, this time at Goshen, New York. During this period he began to compile text-books for the schools and of these he published several. One, a speller, was so successful that it supported him and his family during the time in which the dictionary was in preparation although the royalty he received was only one cent per volume. This book is still in use and more than sixty-two million copies have been printed.

He gave support to the first movement toward a constitution in 1784 and his articles on this question were widely read and had great influence. The same was true of other writings on political subjects including his articles sustaining the Jay treaty ten years later.

He prepared a "Philosophical and Practical Grammar" which was not very successful but it was not until 1807 when he was forty-nine years old that he entered upon the great work of his life, the "American Dictionary of the English Language." This monumental labor required twenty-one years for completion. During this time his studies carried him to the continent of Europe and to England where the work was finally finished. In 1828 an American edition of 2,500 copies was published and was followed by an edition of 3,000 in England.

In 1812 he moved with his family to the town of Amherst, Massachusetts. He was instrumental there in establishing Amherst College and became its first president.

The Connecticut houses which we have described are noticeably similar to those of Massachusetts, such differences as there are being in detail and not in fundamentals. The early types persisted much later in Connecticut than in Massachusetts and in Connecticut there is an almost complete absence of the transitional stage represented by the square three story frame and brick mansions, with classical decoration, so characteristic of northern Massachusetts.

This architectural conservatism was an expression of the attitude of the people and their government. The early leaders of Connecticut were characterized by piety tempered with wisdom. Their conceptions of government were democratic as opposed to the class domination of the mother colony. The result of these tendencies was a greater liberality in both government and religion as compared with Massachusetts and New Haven. As time went on, however, Massachusetts profited by the example of her younger neighbor and from this and other liberalizing influences became the readier to accept new ideas. This is illustrated by the movement in Massachusetts which resulted in the change from the Puritan doctrine to the more liberal tenets of Unitarianism, while in Connecticut the rise of Jonathan Edwards had a tendency to assimilate Congregationalism to the doctrines most rigidly Calvinistic.

There were limits, however, to conservatism even in Connecticut and when Edwards waxed more severe in admissions to his church he was removed by his congregation and was compelled to take up missionary work with the Berkshire Indians. Somewhat later he was called to the Presidency of Princeton College and transferred to New Jersey the preaching and the practice of his austere doctrine.

In this earlier period two men stand out as having most enriched the development of the colony. From the arrival in 1636 until his death Thomas Hooker controlled the religious teaching of the three towns; but not only did he control religious thinking but by the principles he taught, he guided the political conceptions of his fellow citizens. In contrast to New Haven, where Davenport sought to enforce orthodoxy from above and failed, Hooker successfully inspired his flock with the principles of co-operation and democracy. In Massachusetts he opposed John Cotton on doctrinal questions and maintained the principles of democracy in argument with the elder Winthrop. The latter addressed him on this subject expressing his opinion that "It is unsafe to refer matters of counsel or judicature to the body of the people." Hooker in his reply affirmed a truth which is now of general acceptance but at that time smacked of radicalism. "In matters . . . which concern the common good a general council chosen by all to transact business which concerns all, I conceive most suitable to rule and most safe for the relief of the whole."

In the Connecticut constitution of 1639 the representatives of the towns are recognized as the source of power and are given the right to meet by themselves if the Governor and Magistrates refuse to call them together.

That Hooker was mainly responsible for the idea fundamental to this constitution seems beyond question. In his famous sermon preached in Hartford in 1638, he enunciates many of its principles, such as, for instance, the "Doctrine No. I" which he defines as follows: "That the choice of public magistrates belongs unto the people by God's own allowance," and again later he says "The foundation of authority is laid firstly in the free consent of the people."

The influence of this man's clear thinking was far reaching. That it was influential in the final emancipation of Massachusetts is generally acknowledged but its effect was not limited to New England and its fundamentals became, as has already been stated, the basis of the Federal Constitution of 1787.

As Hooker's life was drawing to a close, John Winthrop, Jr., among the younger men, came nearest to taking his place. Winthrop's talent, however, was that of the student rather than of the statesman, his temperament that of the diplomat rather than that of the teacher. In his father, the Governor of Massachusetts, intelligence of a high character and the political wisdom of his class, which was essentially aristocratic, were limited by orthodoxy, but the son seemingly suffered from no such limitation and wisdom in him was tempered by a spirit of co-operation which brought success in all his undertakings and made him the most generally beloved of the public men of his time.

Under the Connecticut constitution the election of governor was annual and the habit arose of making the governor of one year the deputy governor of the next, since re-election to the same office was prohibited. Winthrop was elected governor in 1657 and deputy in 1658. In 1659 he was again made governor and in that year the General Court removed the provision against re-election and thereafter he was continued in office until his death in 1676.

His most notable achievement was the charter obtained from Charles II, reference to which has already been made. An entire winter was devoted to this task and that his time was well spent is proved by the outcome. In his negotiations

with the government and at the court his natural qualities developed through education and travel made him
eminently successful. He was not only accepted by the
court but was recognized as one of the foremost natural
philosophers of his time by contemporary men of letters.
In chemistry and medicine he was particularly skilful and
his advice was sought far and wide. He was one of the first
members of the Royal Society.

His loyalty to his adopted country was sufficiently strong
to induce him to forego the satisfaction of contact with other
cultured intellects, so dear to the student, and to return
to the undeveloped communities to whom his services were
infinitely valuable. To Connecticut he devoted the remainder of his life, esteemed by all, even by those with
whom he differed. His rule as governor was marked by
moderation in judgment and liberality in matters religious.
By the Quakers he was loved for his mercy and by the Indians he was revered for his justice.

The expansion of Plymouth as a colony took place nor-
mally from the center outward towards the west and the
south, although many of the colonists migrated as indi-
viduals to the Connecticut valley, to the north shore of Massachusetts Bay and even along the Maine coast to the border
of Acadia. Its natural expansion developed slowly. The
rapid growth which followed the founding of Salem along the
north shore was not typical of the mother colony. Plymouth
did not to the same extent attract the contentious and the
progressive thought, nor was her shore so well supplied with
harbors to shelter the shipping from the home ports.

During the seventy years of her existence Plymouth maintained her identity as an essentially democratic and toler-

ant community though toward the close of the period her tolerance became somewhat dimmed through contact with Massachusetts Bay. The Pilgrims were an industrious and frugal people inspired not only to support their families in reasonable comfort but also with "a great hope and inward zeal . . . of laying some good foundation . . . for the propagation and advancement of the gospel of Christ in these remote parts of the world."

Materially speaking, they prospered and within fifteen years of the landing had reached westward to the border of the present Rhode Island, north to include Scituate and toward the south they had begun to reach out to the sand dunes of Cape Cod. In 1637 the town of Sandwich was founded by families from Saugus, Duxbury and Plymouth. Two years later Yarmouth was established by Anthony Thatcher who four years previous had been cast away with his wife on the island now known as Thatcher's Island off Cape Ann where husband and wife were protected from the storms by a covering of embroidered scarlet broadcloth which is still in existence and treasured as a family heirloom.

The same year, lands in Barnstable were granted to the Rev. John Lothrop who came from Scituate with twenty-five families. Lothrop, holding a living under the church of England, had been imprisoned as an independent for two years and, released in 1634, had crossed to New England on the same ship with Mrs. Anne Hutchinson.

Eastham was founded five years later (*i.e.*, 1644) by Thomas Prince, a Mayflower Pilgrim, whose first wife was the daughter of Elder Brewster. He was later elected governor of the colony and restored to Plymouth. Settlements extended no further for the time being and it was not until

1727 that the Province lands of the Cape were incorporated as Provincetown.

The Cape took an active part in King Philip's War and John Gorham of Barnstable was in command of their forces. When Plymouth was finally made a part of Massachusetts Bay by the royal charter of William and Mary the character of the imigration changed and it is to the group of Scotch-Irish Presbyterians who came over during the last years of the XVIIth century that the Cape owes the peculiar flavor of its native stock which has set it apart from the rest of Massachusetts.

After the death of John Robinson, and under the influence of the Bay, Plymouth drifted away from his wise and tolerant teaching. When Roger Williams made his first visit to Plymouth he found the elders there but little less rigid than at Boston; but he did find the existing relations with the Indians on a firmer basis than in the north, and was able during his sojourn to establish the friendship with Massasoit which was so valuable in the development of Rhode Island. When, therefore, Providence Plantations came into existence it was there and to Williams rather than to Plymouth that the persecuted turned as to a haven of rest.

This applied most particularly to the Quakers, many of whom had chosen Plymouth as a degree less rigorous than the Bay. The Cape at this time bore eloquent testimony to the fact that the religious idea waxes stronger and gains increased converts under persecution. Copeland and Holden, Quakers, as an example, were publicly whipped in Sandwich, by order of the selectmen, but the result of this ignominy was that eighteen Sandwich families became converted to the despised sect.

The Stephen Wing house of Sandwich, one of the oldest homesteads on the Cape, still stands as witness to a similar persecution.

Stephen, son of the Rev. John W. and Deborah Wing, landed in Boston in 1632 and with his family came to Sand-

The Stephen Wing House.   Sandwich, Cape Cod.

wich in 1637. Four years later he built this home which has remained in the Wing family without transfer until the present time and is now occupied by the representative of the tenth generation. Stephen Wing was a pioneer member of the first Friends Meeting in America founded at Spring Hill, near Sandwich, in 1658. He suffered deeply at the hands of the government of Plymouth in the cause of religious liberty but survived and prospered and founded the family which has multiplied and spread over the country. He died in 1710, fifty-two years after the establishment of the Meeting House and is buried at Spring Hill.

As the continued residence of the family the house has undergone many changes dictated by the tastes of its various owners but has never lost the character of a Cape family home. The hall and the parlor have been left practically intact. The hall has some very fine paneling and wide window seats. The room in the lean-to originally running the full length has been divided into a dining room and a kitchen. There are now, therefore, four rooms on the ground floor in place of the original three. The fireplaces have been closed up and Franklin or other type stoves added for greater comfort in winter.

The Wing family holds its reunions in this house annually.

The John Gorham house of Barnstable, built between 1685–90, is similar to the older John Dillingham house of West Brewster described in Chapter III except for the lean-to. It is of record however, that this house also had a lean-to in the early days which a later generation removed.

James Gorham of Benifield, Northamptonshire, England, married Desire, daughter of John Howland of Plymouth, one of the last survivors of the *Mayflower*. The young couple lived first at Plymouth, shortly after 1646 in Marshfield, and in 1652 moved to Yarmouth which adjoins Barnstable. Here he owned a grist mill and wharf and a tannery. He was deputy to the General Court and held various town offices. His son John, built this house at about the date mentioned. His notable service to his country was in leading the Cape levies to the war in Narragansett, mentioned heretofore. In the final battle December 19, 1675, he was distinguished by his bravery, but due to the hardships of the campaign and to a fever contracted during his enlistment he passed away during the year following. His son, John

The John Gorham House. Barnstable, Cape Cod.

Gorham, Jr., married in 1671 Mary, daughter of John Otis, and was representative of his district in the General Court for several years following 1688. He served in the expedition against Canada in 1690 under Sir William Phips, for which he was made a lieutenant colonel. The family in the early XVIIIth century was one of the best known on the Cape and John's uncle James was reputed to be the

richest man in the countryside.   John's son obtained a grant
of land in Maine and established there the town since known
as Gorham, Maine.   Lieut. Governor John Gorham of a
later generation in 1716 willed the house and lands, called
"Stony Cove," to his son Shubail.   This descendant and
his sons took part in the siege of Louisburg.

The chimney of the old house has been rebuilt, the original
lean-to has been removed, and the exterior has been restored,
but the original lines remain.   Inside we find the shallow
entry and the old framing exposed with chamfered summers.
Simple but excellent paneling and hand tooled moldings of
the early XVIIIth century have been left in the lower rooms.
The shutters and window seats are of the same period.

The house has never been transferred and is still occupied by the family descendants.

The old Atwood house of Chatham is an excellent example of the familiar type, the single chimney, gambrel-roof,
dwelling, so common in early Plymouth days.   This house was
built by Joseph Atwood, descendant of a Stephen Atwood of
Plymouth, in 1752.   He was a ship master of his day and the
ancestor of a long line of Atwoods who have lived and multiplied in and about Chatham and who have, until recently,
continued to occupy the house.   The interior has some good
doors with their HL hinges, an excellent niche and simple
paneling and cupboards about the fireplaces.   The property
has now been purchased with the aid of a popular subscrip-
tion by the Chatham Historical Society and will be preserved as an excellent example of the period and used as a
colonial museum.

The Hallet-Thatcher house of Yarmouth, built in 1730,
represents two of the oldest and most important Cape

families. Andrew Hallett appears as a citizen of Yarmouth in 1639. In 1642 Anthony Thatcher, who founded Yarmouth three years earlier, was a member of the council

The Atwood House. Chatham, Cape Cod.

of war and of the military company of which Miles Standish was captain.

Both Hallett and Thatcher were on the list of those liable to bear arms in 1643, while a year later it is noted that Anthony Thatcher is the one person in Yarmouth licensed to draw wine. In 1655 Thatcher was also commissioned to join in marriage those who so aspired. In 1672 Andrew Hallett appears on the Committee for land grants and eight years later he died.

The Hallett-Thatcher House. Yarmouth, Cape Cod.

A later descendant, Peter Thatcher, became chief justice in 1728 and his daughter, Thankful, married John Hallett. This house was undoubtedly built for the young people. The ell was built somewhat later than the main building and has been used as a post office and store. The main building has three rooms on the ground floor. At present there is no stair in the front entry. Of the three fireplaces, the largest is in the rear room which is used as a kitchen. This room is paneled throughout and has excellent old doors and hinges. The stairway to the upper story now runs from the kitchen.

In this Hallett-Thatcher house we have the Cape Cod type in all its purity and simplicity. Center chimney, one and one half stories with the roof of equal pitch and length front and back without dormers. The dormers are the besetting temptation in remodeling or copying these old houses, as they add much to the second story in head room, light and space, but they are not found in the original houses.

The essential charm of the Cape is its simplicity, expressed in simple farm homesteads, substantial and harmonious but without decoration, in contrast to the aristocratic leanings of the north shore.

The native of the Cape has been farmer, miller, boat builder, seaman, fisherman and ship master, but withal he has ever been a home builder. Cape Cod is famed for its cranberries, fitting condiment for that Thanksgiving feast founded at Plymouth after the first meager harvest but forerunner of the mighty repasts that their descendants have joyfully consumed in their memory. Twenty-five years after the first Thanksgiving, Bradford wrote: "Nor has there been any general want of food among us since, to this day."

Cape Cod is doing its best to maintain the tradition of its forefathers by providing against that day of want, which, according to its calculations, is the last Thursday of November.

APE Ann and its adjacent territory were fairly well known in England many years before a permanent settlement was made on the peninsula. Information regarding the country had been brought back by Gosnold who sailed past the Cape in 1602; by John Smith who explored the coast to a point considerably farther north in 1614 and by many fishing voyages to the Island of Monhegan whose crews had pretty well explored the coast line. An abundance of fish was reported and it was to take advantage of this fruitful supply that the Merchant Adventurers risked their capital and the lives of their associates. The Dorchester Company was incorporated to establish a plantation in the new world where agriculture and other business could be undertaken and from which successful voyages for fish could be started. A single ship of fifty tons burthen sailed from England in 1623 with Cape Ann as its destination and with this object in view. The Rev. John White of Dorchester was its leader and one Humphrey the treasurer of the Adventurers. Mr. White has left us a full account of this first adventure in "The Planter's Plea on the Grounds of Plantations examined and usual Objections Answered. Together with a Manifestation of the Causes moving such as have lately Undertaken a Plantation in New England," published in London in 1630.

No religious purpose actuated this settlement although those engaged in it were of the Puritan persuasion. The undertaking itself was concerned purely with trade. The program provided that a fishing vessel should be double manned so that in the fishing season fish could be caught and handled more promptly than with the ordinary ship's crew and that when the fishing was finished one half of the crew could be left to plant corn and other farm products while the vessel sailed for a foreign port with its cargo. It was expected that with supplies left with the planters and such venison as they could take sufficient subsistence could be had until the following spring when the operation would be repeated.

Gloucester in this manner took its beginning as a fishing port in 1623 and has not materially varied since from this purpose for which it was founded.

Three thousand pounds were subscribed and paid in by the Adventurers. The investment, however, turned out to be an unprofitable one for them. The first cargo was secured in Massachusetts Bay and carried to Spain while fourteen men with the necessary provisions were left "in the countrie at Cape Ann" to establish the Plantation. The expense of this first voyage including the cost of the vessel ran to eight hundred pounds and two hundred pounds only were returned to the Company.

Cape Ann was at this period of its history an isolated and remote post. The only substantial settlement on the coast was at Plymouth. A few settlers at Nantasket and the remnant of the Gorges Plantation at Weymouth were their nearest neighbors. In this same year a few settlers also established themselves at the Piscataqua River and at

Saco. A company also had landed on Monhegan Island. These with a few scattering settlements on the coast of Maine comprised then the total of English emigration to New England.

Two of the Pilgrims, Edward Winslow and Robert Cushman, obtained from Lord Sheffield, a member of the Council for New England, at about this time also a patent "in a known place there commonly called Cape Anne." Fishing was also the object of this undertaking. The two groups worked together apparently in harmony for about three years and both then withdrew from the undertaking for the same reason, that is, the lack of profit in the enterprise. Five vessels, however, arrived from England in 1625 and salt pans and fishing stages were established both by the Dorchester Company and by Plymouth. But with the close of this year's fishing Plymouth withdrew and the men of the Dorchester Company returned to England. Roger Conant, who, with a few followers had been invited to join the community from Nantasket resolved to stay and took over the equipment of the Dorchester Company. The year following he also found it impracticable to hold on longer at this remote and exposed point and retired to Naumkeag which was shortly to become the town of Salem. In view of these events Gloucester can claim the distinction of having within its borders the spot on which the colony of Massachusetts Bay was founded. This spot has been known as "Fisherman's Field" and is located on the northwest side of the outer harbor near which the landing stage is still known as "the Stage."

The Rev. John White encouraged Conant to remain at Naumkeag until Endicott and his company arrived in 1628.

In 1630 came the large emigration under Winthrop which firmly planted the colony. Three years after this several of the Winthrop emigration re-established the post at Cape Ann but it was not until 1642 that the Rev. Richard Blynman with several families from Plymouth settled this point on a firm foundation as a permanent Plantation. It was named Gloucester, since several of the settlers hailed from Gloucester on the river Severn.

Fishing continued as the industry of the settlers and ship building was added as a natural development of an essentially seafaring people.

An interesting contract is in existence signed by William Stevens, a shipwright and "John Brown for himself and Nicholas and John Balbach of Jersey to build one new ship of 68 feet long by ye keele and 23 feet broad in ye hold under beam with two decks, fore castle, quarter deck . . . said Stevens to be paid three pounds five shillings for every tun of said ships burthen." Part of the payment was to be made by "One hundred and fifty pounds in muscovados shugar at two pence by the pound at Barbadoes." [1]

In the early years of the XVIIIth century the town greatly enlarged its activity in ship building and other industries pertaining to the seafaring life of its citizens and definitely entered upon its career as a deep sea fishing port whose fleet annually assembled on the Grand Banks to supply the raw material of its factors who, in turn, distributed their product to all parts of the world.

Gloucester, though founded in the first instance for trade alone, was re-established by settlers from Plymouth and emigrants of the Puritan party from England. Its build-

[1] "Town of Gloucester, Cape Ann and Rockport," by John J. Babson.

ing, therefore, followed the general line of development of the rest of Massachusetts Bay though it partook rather of the style of rural Massachusetts than of adjacent cities such as Salem and Newburyport where the profits of foreign trade formed the basis of aristocratic living which expressed

The Davis-Freeman House.   West Gloucester, Mass.

itself in the sumptuous Georgian mansions of the end of the XVIIIth century.

The Davis-Freeman house of West Gloucester, probably the oldest building standing in this locality, is, as will be noted, of the oblong, two and a half story type without lean-to but with framed overhang of the second story on three sides as well as the gable.   From the remains of the carved brackets it is evident that this originally was a house of some elegance, similar in type to the Parson Capen house of Topsfield. Neither its original date nor its early history are known but expert opinion places its construction as "well before 1700." It has for some years been used

The White-Ellery House. Gloucester, Mass.

as a tenement and the interior cut up into small rooms has lost its ancient character. It is rapidly falling to pieces and failing the attention of some lover of old houses will shortly disappear.

The White-Ellery house faces south with its east end on the highway which is the extension of Middle Street and at its back is the stretch of upland which was Gloucester's original Green and the spot where stood the first Meeting House.

The homestead was built in 1704 for the Rev. John White, descendant of the Rev. John White of the Dorchester Company, previously mentioned, as the first parsonage, since the younger John White was the pastor of its first Parish church. He was a graduate of Harvard of the class of 1678 and when called to Gloucester was chaplain of the Saco fort.

In 1738 it was bought by James Stevens and used for some time as a tavern. Later in its history it fell into the hands of Captain William Ellery, one of the selectmen and a man prominent in the town's affairs, and was for many years the center where much of the town's business was transacted. The Ellery family has continuously lived in it since and it is now the home of the sixth and seventh generations. In this old homestead we have the familiar two and a half story, central chimney, lean-to type of the period, with a wide overhang. The house has been kept in excellent repair and its original lines are unchanged.

Across the street from the White-Ellery house, its lawn bordered with a fence festooned with pink roses, stands the Babson house, a more elegant mansion of the next generation. This house was built for Joseph Allen's son in 1738-40. There was a William Allen, one of the Adventurers who came to Cape Ann for the Dorchester Company from whom this Joseph Allen may have descended. The latter, however, is known to have been a blacksmith and that he was induced to settle in Gloucester in 1674 by a grant of land and a common right. The house a little later came to the Babson family with whom it has remained and is now the home of the sixth or seventh generation.

In spite of many changes in the style of the house, the original central chimney has been retained with its shallow

The Babson House. Gloucester, Mass.

entry in front. The stairway runs from right to left against the chimney. Its baluster and spindles have been changed to accord with the Georgian decorations of the ground floor rooms. The parlor (left) was made over and quite modernized in 1800 to welcome a bride. The west entrance was also added at this time. The hall, however, is completely paneled, with summer encased and has one of the most beautiful niches seen in this part of the country. The paneling is unusually good, probably added after 1760, its style distinctly the English classic. The rear room originally had a large fireplace which has been partially bricked up. Part of this back room was used as a cobbler's workshop and the part that remained as living quarters for the slaves. The ell on the east end was added about 1800 and the present portico within a few years.

The Judith Sargent house down in the center of the town, was built by Winthrop Sargent about 1768 for his daughter Judith who was first the wife of John Stevens and later married John Murray, the founder of Universalism in America. It was during his incumbency that the right to free worship was contested in the courts and the verdict rendered in favor of religious liberty.

The house has changed hands many times during its century and a half of existence and has been the home of many well-known Gloucester families, including the Rev. Samuel Gilman, the author of "Fair Harvard," who was born here in 1791. John Singer Sargent, America's best-known portrait painter, is of this family and the Sargent room contains many of his sketches besides copies of portraits of Judith Sargent by Copley and Gilbert Stuart as well as other family portraits.

In 1915 the property was purchased by the Sargent-Murray-Gilman Association and the house is being restored under the supervision of Mr. Joseph Everett Chandler of Boston and will be preserved for the benefit of future generations. This dwelling is an interesting specimen of Geor-

The Judith Sargent House.   Gloucester, Mass.

gian pre-Revolutionary mansion of the same period as the Hamilton house of South Berwick, Maine. Attached to the rear of the square main building is an ell, doubtless a later addition, with an entrance on the street. This ell and the main building are divided into many small rooms which suggest the additions of different generations and the varying tastes of its owners. The interior loses something of general effect through this diversity. Its main hall is narrow and although it has a fine stairway with mahogany rail, carved spindles and newel post, it lacks the spaciousness and dignity of the Hamilton or the Wentworth-Gardner houses. The rooms on the second floor also are somewhat contracted and lack general effect. The house is notable, however, for very beautiful paneling which is used to a greater or less extent on both floors and in the wainscoting of the stairway.

Marblehead has also drawn its livelihood and the inspiration of its sailor folk from the hazardous though fiber-strengthening enterprise of fishing on the Grand Banks. Settled in 1629, the first emigrants are believed to have been fishermen from Guernsey and Jersey who, for generations had followed the sea. The town itself, piled up on its little hills, abutting the base of Marblehead Neck, has much the flavor of the fishing villages along the coasts of Devon and of Cornwall and like them its annals are filled with rescues on a rugged coast and courageous battling with the sea in days of peace and the manning of privateers in time of war—a life of adventure and strenuous endeavor which makes strong men and faithful women. Marblehead takes pardonable pride in the courage and loyalty of her citizens. In every war with which the country has been afflicted the men of Marblehead have been the first to volunteer. In the early XVIIIth century the shipments of dried cod from this port were the largest of any point along the coast and in the years preceding the Revolution a hundred of her fishing boats on the average sailed twice a year to the Grand Banks.

All this has passed away, nought but the lobster pots

remain and most of the typical old houses have gone with the deep sea fishing, swallowed up by tearooms or absorbed into summer cottages.

The "Old Brig" is recognized as one of the most ancient buildings left standing though neither its exact age nor the

The Old Brig. Marblehead, Mass.

name of its builder are definitely known. The present owner credits it to Moses Maverack. It undoubtedly dates from some time before 1700 and in its construction follows the lines of other old oblong, two story, single chimney houses without lean-to, common to the North Shore, examples of which we have already discussed. The name "Old Brig" signifies that the original hewn oak timbers with which it is framed were taken from the wreck of an old brigantine. It is located on the sharp turn of Orne Street as it leads to the Burying Hill and is therefore in the oldest part of the town.

We have already described the efforts, many times renewed, of Massachusetts to gain control of the settlements about the Piscataqua River and of the character of the early emigration to these towns and to the posts along the Maine coast. Captain John Mason was one of the first merchants in England to become interested in trading in New England. Originally a London merchant, he became a ship master and engaged in the Newfoundland fishing and was appointed Governor of that Island. On his return to England he was appointed Governor of Portsmouth in Hampshire and made secretary of the Plymouth Council created by royal decree "For the planting, ruling, ordering and governing of New England in America." By this council he was given a grant for "all the land from the river Naumkeag (Salem) round Cape Anne to the river Merrimack and up each of these rivers to the farthest head thereof then to cross over from the head of the one to the head of the other with all the islands lying within three miles of the coast." This took place in 1621, only a year after the landing of the Pilgrims at Plymouth. The territory he named "Mariana." In the year following, the council granted to Mason and Sir Ferdinando Gorges jointly "all lands situated between the rivers Merrimack and Sagadehuck extending back to the Great Lakes and the river of Canada" and called it Laconia. They admitted as associates several other merchants of London, Bristol, Exeter, Plymouth, Shrewsbury and Dorchester and styled themselves "The Company of Laconia." A year later the company sent over David Thompson, a Scotchman, Edward Hilton and Thomas Hilton his brother, fishmongers of London and others to establish a plantation and a business in fish at the mouth of the Piscataqua.

In 1629 a purchase of much of the same territory was made of the Indians by John Wheelright, William Wentworth and others, and John Mason obtained a new grant from the Council of Plymouth while the Council extended the grant made to the colony of Massachusetts Bay to three miles north of the Merrimack River, and so the patents continually interfered with one another.

The settlements about the mouth of the river did not thrive and within five years the other proprietors became discouraged with the results from the Plantation and sold their interests to Gorges and Mason. These two subsequently made a division of the property held in common and Gorges relinquished his right to lands in New Hampshire but retained his proprietorship of Maine. Mason advanced large sums without much return. Although he invested in the hope of profit yet in so doing he made an early settlement of the country possible. He, himself, never came to New Hampshire. In 1637, a government was established by the settlers themselves around the Piscataqua, so that from 1641–44 there were four separate Republics on the river, namely Portsmouth, Kittery, Dover and Exeter. The towns asked to be taken over by Massachusetts and this was accomplished by contract drawn up and signed before the General Court in 1642. Massachusetts' law, requiring Freemen who voted in town meeting to be church members, was omitted under the contract as applying to these New Hampshire towns.

The Piscataqua settlers were not Puritans but members of the Church of England. Their first rector, Richard Gibson, a Church of England clergyman gave offense to Massachusetts Bay and shortly returned to England. Later on, though still holding to the Church of England, to conciliate Massachusetts, they called the Rev. James Parker of Weymouth as their pastor and still later Thomas Dudley, son of the Deputy Governor of Massachusetts.

A few years later, under the Commonwealth, Massachusetts extended her rule to Maine and though taken from her temporarily, the Puritans outwitted Charles by purchasing the rights of Gorges' grandson and the eventual inclusion of Maine in her territory took place through the charter granted by King William. New Hampshire was at the same time made a Royal Province. For many years after the enactment of the royal charter for Massachusetts and New Hampshire the Crown made the Governor of Massachusetts the acting Governor of New Hampshire. This left in the hands of Massachusetts the control of the entire coast as far north as English rule extended. Her territory was too extended and the organization of government too undeveloped to permit such long range control and the settlements about the Piscataqua suffered much from lack of protection and the proper training of the citizens for defense. In the year 1739, Benning Wentworth, of Portsmouth, a member of the Royal Council is found petitioning the Crown for relief indicating the defenseless condition of the harbor and the River Piscataqua and pointing out that the Province which was then supplying the Royal Navy with masts, might readily fall a prey to French or Indian attack. The people were much aroused over the lack of government furnished by Massachusetts and the result of their activity was the complete separation of New Hampshire from Massachusetts and the removal of Belcher who was then Governor of Massachusetts and the appointment of William Shirley to succeed him in that office while

The Jackson House. Rear. Portsmouth, N. H.

Benning Wentworth his chief opponent in New Hampshire was appointed Governor of the latter province. Belcher was, presumably, placated by a later appointment as Governor of New Jersey. This change resulted in larger achievements than the petitioners themselves had anticipated.

One of the few homesteads standing in the Piscataqua territory which dates from the XVIIth century is the Jackson house, located in the district called Christian Shore of Portsmouth. It was built in 1664 by Richard Jackson, facing south on a slope running to an arm of the Bay, as were most of the original dwellings, since at that time water was the most satisfactory means of communication.   The prop-

The Jackson House.   Front.   Portsmouth, N. H.

erty was originally of twenty-six acres and was entailed so that it has remained in the same family until a year ago when the entail was broken by the representative of the ninth generation and the house sold to the Society for the Preservation of New England Antiquities.

The lean-to, as shown in the photograph of the rear, is unusually low and extends to the ground. This was the first addition, the eastern ell the second and the western lean-to the most recent. An humble dwelling from the beginning, its stairway rising from its shallow entry is boarded up and is without rail or spindles. The chimney throughout is constructed of brick which were presumably imported, as bricks were not made in the colony at that early period. The girth timbers are unusually large, at least sixteen inches square. In the lean-to there is a curious domed brick oven where baking was done. There are, therefore, but two fireplaces on the ground floor. The last addition covered up most of the west windows leaving the west chamber almost dark. The hall is equipped with a wide baseboard of pine, perhaps twenty-four inches wide, reaching to the floor to protect this living room from the dust and cold which would naturally seep in from the lean-to. The house is an excellent example of the simple fisherman's home in a community which turned very early to construction of a much more substantial character. It is fortunate that, for our instruction, it has been preserved to remind us of its humble beginnings. The plaster and wall paper have been scraped off the old timbers in the parlor and hall but no further effort as yet has been made toward its restoration.

The part of Portsmouth named "Christian Shore" was, in the town books of the early XVIIIth century, called "The land on the other side of Strawberry Bank Creek," but the Jackson family and their neighbors of Puritan stock, were of a stricter attitude than the townspeople across the inlet where one Foss kept a tavern. Foss' ale of brown October brew was famed far and wide and his votaries lingered over their cups often beyond the hour which would have been permitted across the Merrimack in Massachu-

setts Bay, and so the roysterers, some of whom dwelt among
the Puritans, came to say when parting from their fellows
at the tavern "Well, we must leave for Christian Shore,"
and thus the name was fixed and, being shorter and more
expressive than the original, has survived to the present
day.[1]

King Philip's War of which we have heard much in Rhode
Island and Connecticut was particularly disastrous to the
northern coast because of its isolation and lack of protection. When Philip finally fell the Penobscot tribe sent the
Sachem Mugg to Boston where he signed a peace treaty.
The next year, however, the war was renewed and the Indians continued their depredations along the coast practically without opposition. In 1678 the settlers made a treaty
with the Indians but were compelled to agree to the humil-
iating condition of paying the tribes a tribute in corn every
year to insure the keeping of the peace.

At the outbreak of Queen Anne's War in 1703, a wholesale slaughter of the settlers that remained emphasized the
close understanding between the French and their Indian
allies. The chief instigator was Father Sebastien Ralle
who had built a chapel at Norridgewalk for the Indians'
use and it was not until his capture and execution in 1724
by Captains Moulton and Harman of York that permanent
settlement became possible.

The result of this continued border warfare was practical obliteration of the settlements from Casco Bay east for
a period of thirty years. Attempts at resettlement were
made in 1714–16 but it was not until 1729 that the English
government sent over Col. David Dunbar as supervisor of

[1] "Rambles about Portsmouth," by George H. Ellis.

the King's woods, to organize new communities, that the beginnings of the present Maine towns took place.

Although the original settlement of Wiscasset which lies a short distance west of Damariscotta was somewhere around 1630, for reasons given in the foregoing, which apply to other Maine towns as well, it has no present buildings earlier than the latter part of the XVIIIth century. We have seen one very good specimen of that period in the Governor Smith house (Chapter III).

The Captain Jack Johnston house, less ornate than that of Governor Smith, was built in 1808. It is the square hip roof, four chimney type characteristic of many of the simpler ship master's mansions along the Maine coast. The owner and the builder, Captain Jack Johnston was captain of many clipper ships, including the *Tamerlane*, the *Sterling*, the *Queen of Sheba* and others. Fennimore Cooper lived for some time with him and it was on voyages of the ship *Sterling* that he had his first sea experiences. It is understood that these adventures, particularly some encounters with pirates incidental to them, furnished him with material for his sea tales to a greater extent than those adventures which he had in later years during his service in the navy.

The house is filled with mementoes, curious or beautiful, the product of voyages to every part of the navigable globe. Access to the second floor is by a circular staircase rising against the wall of a well running to the roof, a change from the broad, square hall of the Georgian mansion, not uncommon in this and later periods. The southeast room has some excellent paneling.

A group of Scotch Irish Presbyterians settled at this point about 1720 and had much to do with the development

of Wiscasset as a port, and their descendants became the
ship masters and owners of a later generation. Of this stock
sprang Captain William Nickels, builder of the mansion
which bears his name. He was both captain and owner of
merchant ships. The export of timber was an important

The Captain Jack Johnston House. Wiscasset, Me.

activity of this port in the XVIIIth century. Masts for
the Royal Navy were furnished from the spruce and pine
tributary to it and to insure the best timber the King's
rangers surveyed the woods and reserved the trees selected
and blazed them with the symbol of an arrow. As industry
developed, the manufacture of barrel staves and shingles
followed with other products made possible by a sawmill
which was established here as early as 1740. As the harbor

The Captain William Nickels House. Wiscasset, Me.

never freezes, shipments of forest products were facilitated throughout the year.

The well designed Georgian mansion of Captain Nickels was for many years used as a tavern under the name of the Wiscasset House. About twenty years ago it was bought by the present owner and restored to its original dignity and elegance.

As Wiscasset marked approximately the eastern limit of English settlement up to the time Acadia was ceded to France, so Hampton was the settlement nearest to the Merrimack River on the west under the Masonian grants. This was one of the towns, as will be recalled, settled by the banished followers of Mrs. Anne Hutchinson. Among the fifty-six original settlers were the ancestors of that Jonathan Moulton who, in a later generation, was Hampton's most notable son. His manor house stands now on a slight eminence facing the Lafayette Road, its harmonious exterior and elaborately paneled chambers restored to the patrician elegance of line and detail designed by the builder.

General Jonathan Moulton was born in 1726. His family had lived in Hampton from its settlement and his descendants have remained in this community until the present time. He married twice and became the father of fifteen children. He was honored for distinguished service to the colony during the Indian wars which ended with the destruction of the Ossipee tribe near Moultonborough. Large grants of land were made to him at various times, doubtless the result of these services and of his knowledge of the frontier over which he had fought. The largest of these was a tract of 19,000 acres, covering territory which now includes New Hampton and Center Harbor, transferred to him by authority of Governor

Benning Wentworth. Four New Hampshire towns owe their inception to his activities: namely, Moultonborough, New Hampton, Center Harbor and Meredith near Concord.

He was several times a representative in the State legislature and served with the rank of Colonel through the Revo-

The General Jonathan Moulton House. Hampton, N. H.

lution. His rank of General was doubtless subsequent to that service. He had built or had owned an earlier house located not far from the present site. This house valued at three thousand pounds, evidently a house of some importance, was burned in 1769, and it is understood that the present house was built immediately after the destruction of the earlier homestead.

The house stood originally across the road from its location on the hillside to which it has been moved by the present owner.

Many romances have clustered about this mansion. Whittier names it the "Haunted House" and tells the story of the two wives in the poem, "The New Wife and the Old." The poet died not far from here in the house of Miss Gove at Hampton Falls. The Gove homestead is a replica of this Moulton house built by the grandfather of Whittier's hostess.

In its square front section this house resembles the Wentworth-Gardner house, which we have described in Chapter III, without its dormers. From internal evidence it seems probable that the rear gambrel ell was an older building to which the square Georgian front was added. The chimneys were not taken down in moving and they and the fireplaces are original. In the restoration nothing has been added and every effort possible has been made to uncover and retain original detail. The ornamentation of the lower windows and the simple but satisfying doorways are in consonance with the dignity and restraint of the design. The front entrance by its unusual width enhances the hospitable effect.

A broad hall divides the main building with a straight stairway of simple line. Four rooms open from this hall on each floor. All have fireplaces, some of which are tiled and all paneled above the mantel. The mantels in the front rooms are of classic outline simply moulded and beaded. In these rooms are built-in window seats and solid sliding shutters. All the rooms in the main building are wainscoted half way and the present owner has finished the upper walls with modern reproductions of colonial papers. The dining room fireplace has its original bake oven but the largest fireplace is in the gambrel ell, used as a kitchen, in which the opening is from ten to eleven feet in width and includes a large oven. The furniture of the mansion includes carefully selected specimens of the period so that the ensemble now faithfully interprets the life of the mid XVIIIth century so far as modern conditions permit.

Two of the most famous homesteads of the Piscataqua country stand on opposite sides of the river near its mouth at about equal distances from the center of Portsmouth. These were the manor houses of the two men who were in their day most prominent in the councils of the colony and of New England. Their careers were closely interwoven with each other in the stirring days of achievement which followed the long period of England's failures—days which prepared this colony, as well as all New England, for its final emancipation.

The William Pepperrell Mansion stands on the south side of the highway at the east end of Kittery and its garden slopes gently to the river as it empties into the Atlantic. It is now a two and one half story gambrel structure with a chimney at each end. Originally the house was thirty-four feet longer than at present. A section of about twenty feet was taken from each end and an addition of about six feet made to the western end (foreground of illustration). The last addition includes the door surmounted by the carved eagle which is understood to have been cut by the woodcarver Bellamy. Enough material was taken from the two earlier reductions to build a new house. The six foot addition to the west end is comparatively recent, probably of the early XIXth century.

The first William Pepperrell, a fisherman by trade, emigrated from Cornwall in England in 1676 and settled on the Isles of Shoals. Without capital but with boundless energy and courage, his trade flourished. After some years of progress he paid his respects to a lady of the islands whom

The William Pepperrell House.   Kittery, Maine

he desired to marry but she, lacking confidence in his ability to maintain a family, repulsed him. Nothing daunted he returned to his fishing and accumulated enough before long to fit out a brig in which he shipped a cargo to Hull. This set him on his feet and renewing his suit he found the lady more kindly disposed. They were married and moved to Kittery where he established himself in the homestead

we are describing. The date of its erection is given as
"after 1662," which would indicate that he found a house
already built and adapted it to his uses. The principal
changes and embellishments in the mansion were undoubtedly made by his son, the baronet, to suit the dignity of
his position and in accord with the classic tendency of the
time and the district.

The elder Pepperrell became prominent in the community;
was made a Colonel of Militia and held various public offices.
He passed from the scene at the ripe old age of eighty-six,
in 1734. His son, William Pepperrell, born in 1696, succeeded him as a merchant and trader, served the public in
many capacities also and was the recipient of many honors.
He was in turn Chief Justice of the Court of Common
Pleas, President of the Council of Massachusetts and Commander in Chief of the Colonial forces. His achievements
in this latter capacity brought him the largest measure of
his fame.

War was declared with France and Spain in 1744. The
colonies, smarting under the continued blows of France and
her Indian allies and England's failures to arrest them,
sought a means of crippling the enemy by an attack on her
strongholds. William Shirley, then Governor of Massachusetts, in examining exchanged prisoners of war who had
been confined at the fortress of Louisburg, became con-
vinced that that important French base, though called
impregnable, could be taken. He proposed that the colonies
of Massachusetts and New Hampshire unite in the undertaking and submit the plan to the home government.
Benning Wentworth, then Governor of New Hampshire,
approved and the home government endorsed the effort

though doubting the result. New Hampshire borrowed thirteen thousand pounds and raised a regiment of four hundred men while Massachusetts went still further with both men and money. Commodore Warren was sent out from England with a squadron of ships.

The post of commander in chief was given to William Pepperrell of Kittery, then a merchant of unblemished reputation, well known and liked in Massachusetts as well as New Hampshire but entirely unskilled in military affairs. The squadron besieged the fortress in the early spring of 1745 and managed not only to shut off supplies to the garrison but to capture valuable cargoes intended for them. The city capitulated on June 17 after two and one half months of siege. The news of the victory was received with amazement in England and corresponding chagrin across the channel that such a feat could have been accomplished by raw militia. The colonies were elated and Pepperrell became the hero of the hour. For England it was the turn of the tide and the government did everything in its power to show its appreciation. Warren was made an Admiral and a Baronet, Pepperrell a Baronet and Shirley and Pepperrell Generals in the British Army. The colonies were also re-imbursed for their expenditures by Parliament.

The present house has the wide hall common to Georgian houses, completely paneled. The paneling is now painted a rather ugly shade of yellow and brown but is said to be of mahogany. The design is excellent. A very beautiful broad stairway with easy risers leads to a landing with a fine Palladian window. Both the front rooms, *i.e.*, those facing the garden, are completely paneled also with rich embellishments of pilasters and other classic ornaments.

On either side of the fireplaces are round topped cupboards.
The general effect of the interior is one of spaciousness and
dignity implying a generous hospitality.

On the south side of the river at a point called Little
Harbor, about two miles from the center of Portsmouth,

The Benning Wentworth House. From the wharf.
Little Harbor, N. H.

is the romantic rambling old mansion of Governor Benning
Wentworth. The oldest part of the house is reputed to
have been built in the XVIIth century but the more important center building was built in 1750 by Governor
Wentworth. The house faces nearly south and is located
on a point of land jutting into the Bay.

Benning Wentworth was the son of Lieut. Governor
John Wentworth and a graduate of Harvard College of the

class of 1715. He engaged in trade and became eminent as a merchant. His largest undertaking was a consignment of native American oak which he sold to the Spanish government. To defray the expense of production and transportation it was necessary to borrow between fifty and sixty thousand pounds. The loan was secured in London. He accompanied the shipment himself and made delivery of the material according to contract but the Spanish authorities refused to make payment. To add to his misfortunes his ship was lost on the return voyage but he and the crew were fortunately rescued. He then applied in England for government aid in collecting his claim against Spain. While negotiations were in progress war was declared. As a result his claim was not paid and subsequently he was compelled to withdraw it.

Through Mr. Tomlinson, his friend at court, he now made application for appointment as Governor of New Hampshire. This appointment was subsequently made at a salary of two hundred and fifty pounds per year, later increased to five hundred, with house rent added. Somewhat later the office of Surveyor of Woods was added to his other duties at an additional salary of eight hundred pounds. Very popular at this time with his fellow citizens in New Hampshire, he was welcomed on his return with every mark of respect and affection. His administration of twenty-five years as Governor is the longest of any of the royal governors and was marked by many and varied achievements. For the attack on Louisburg, to the command of which he appointed Lieut. Pepperrell, as already mentioned, he was active in recruiting troops and gave his full support to the voting of colonial funds.

The Benning Wentworth House. Front View. Little Harbor, N. H.

It was his purpose to establish a college for the colony but failing an agreement with those interested, as to its management, he gave five hundred acres of land to Hanover, N. H., on which the buildings of Dartmouth College have since been erected.

His Tory leanings consequent upon his position and training brought him into conflict with the colonists as the crisis with the home government approached, and in 1766 his resignation as Governor was accepted. He was succeeded by his nephew, John Wentworth. After his death in 1770 his widow married Col. Michael Wentworth of the English branch of the family who had come over from England shortly before. When General Washington went to Portsmouth in 1789, he made a visit to the mansion by water and was entertained by Col. Michael Wentworth and his wife.

The story of the marriage of Gov. Benning Wentworth with his housekeeper, Martha Hilton is told by Longfellow as one of the Tales of a Wayside Inn.

The main entrance, shown at the right of the front view, leads through a small vestibule into a hall with a straight staircase parallel to the front of the house. This appears to be the oldest part of the house and includes the present dining room and kitchen. Adjoining this old part is the section containing the famous Council Chamber (middle section, second illustration). At the entrance to it, the racks remain for the muskets of the Governor's guard. The studding of this large square room is unusually high for a house of this type and the height of ceiling added to its size makes it unexpectedly impressive after the modest exterior and entrance. On the west side is a large fireplace surmounted by a carved marble chimney piece running to the ceiling, which gives an ornate, sumptuous effect to the room. Adjoining this room are the ancient billiard and card rooms for the entertainment of the Governor's guests, in one of which still stand the old spinet and the corner buffet. The ell which opens out of these rooms (right of second illustration) has been added within the past twenty years by the present owner.

In this unusual mansion, therefore, we have a dignified and formal chamber, well suited to the purpose for which it was intended, which one might expect to find in a town hall or at least in a Georgian mansion such as the Warner house, set in the midst of a low, comfortable, rambling house which partakes much more in its general lines of the XVIIth than of the XVIIIth century.

In this Council Chamber the Governor held the official meetings of the Council during the entire period of his administration and in it business of prime importance to the colony and to the future nation was transacted.

The house has two wings in the rear or north side with a court or garden between them. In the Governor's time the house was larger than at present though which section has been reduced is not disclosed. One of its curiosities is a huge cellar in which the Governor kept his horses at times and which at a pinch could accommodate a troop of cavalry.

Under the curious jog in the main roof was originally a kind of roof terrace or garden which was later removed and covered with the present odd shaped ell. The whole forms a picturesque and bizarre sky line, not unpleasing to the eye and suggestive of the varied and checkered history of its occupants.

CHAPTER VII

WHALING AND THE QUAKERS

MERICAN whaling may be said to have taken its beginning on the beaches of Southampton and Easthampton, Long Island, and from these exposed shores the harpooning of whales from small boats was first projected as a community enterprise. Early in the XVIIIth century, however, Nantucket fitted out ships for the deep sea fishing of sperm whales and developed it into an important industry. By the end of the century she was sending to sea a hundred and fifty whalers a year and the entire community was absorbed in their equipment.

The forty years between the Revolution and the War of 1812 were the most difficult for the New England ship masters since the seas were then barred to American shipping by English guns. During this period whaling languished all along the coast.

Following the War of 1812, New Bedford, an offshoot of Nantucket in deep sea whale fishing, began to outdistance her leader and her shipping marked the high tide of whaling during the succeeding period, between 1840 and 1850, when, at her wharves were fitted out annually no less than two hundred and fifty ships for this purpose.

The typical whalers were mostly barks, that is, ships fitted with square sails on the foremast and mainmast and a leg-of-mutton or schooner rig sail on the mizzen mast.

They ran from 400 to 500 tons burden, from 100 feet to 120 feet in length and from 25 feet to 30 feet beam. A half size model of the bark *Lagoda* in the Bourne Me morial Building in New Bedford preserves for future generations the complete and detailed equipment of these vessels which are now rapidly disappearing from the seas.

The usual voyage included a stop at the Azores and a course along the west coast of Africa to the Cape of Good Hope. From the Cape the route lay across the Indian Ocean to Australia and from Australian ports north to Behring Sea. At times the voyage culminated at off shore grounds in the central Pacific and captains generally stopped at the Polynesian Islands to barter for supplies. Many discoveries of islands hitherto unknown to Europe or American were incidental to these voyages. The route homeward led *via.* Cape Horn and north in the Atlantic. The product of the catch was divided between the owners and the crew and the entire population of the port from which she sailed was interested directly or indirectly in the result of her voyage. While some ships were off on their long voyages others were either leaving or returning and their equipment furnished occupation for sail makers, coopers, blacksmiths and rope makers. The whaling communities were prosperous and contented and were possessed of a knowledge of world affairs due to the frequent voyages of their young men, uncommon at the present day.

Whaling dominated the activities of the New Bedford territory from the middle of the XVIIIth century until the discovery of petroleum in 1869 made an end to the industry as an activity of national importance. Even now the odor of sperm oil is not entirely absent from the water front and occasionally in these days a small whaler is fitted out to hunt the sperm whale off Cape Hatteras. In her beginnings, however, New Bedford like other parts of Massachusetts was a farming community.

A grant of land was made in 1652 to thirty-six "Old Comers," *i.e.*, original settlers, of Plymouth which extended across the head waters of the three rivers which flow into Buzzards Bay through the New Bedford region. The territory was incorporated twelve years later as Dartmouth, a square tract about fourteen miles each way crossing the three rivers, so that the town included four promontories separated by streams which were not fordable within four miles of the Bay.

Four years after the first grant there arose in Massachusetts the persecution of the Quakers which drove many of that inclination to Roger Williams and the friendly islands of Narragansett Bay. As a result, the islands in the Bay became overcrowded and many Quakers purchased land in the western end of Dartmouth from the Plymouth grantees who had not occupied their holdings. The two western towns, therefore, became solidly Quaker, while those on the eastern border followed Plymouth as Puritan communities. Each town by law was compelled to maintain a Meeting House and this fact brought about a division of the original town for religious reasons. The Quakers for many years protested the payment of tithes to support a Puritan Meeting House to which they were held by the Puritan minority and were finally released from this burden by royal decree shortly before the Revolution.

The Puritans on their side had many causes of complaint. Particularly they questioned the sincerity of the Quakers

on the subject of war and when the Revolution broke out
they openly accused them of Toryism in refusing to par-
ticipate.

The many differences arising from these points of view
so fundamentally opposed to each other, made the dwelling
together in harmony of the two elements an impossibility
and a complete and final divorce became the only satisfactory solution. The separation of Dartmouth into its
integral parts did not take place all at once, however.
Westport and Dartmouth were cut off first, leaving New
Bedford and the two eastern towns together. The separation
of these sections by the wide river made their continuing
union difficult and finally Acushnet and Fairhaven were
cut off from New Bedford and separated from each other.
The great majority of the population up to the time of the
Revolution was Quaker in sentiment and it is not surprising,
therefore, that this sect brought with it from Aquidneck
the style of building there adopted, leaving to the settlers
of Fairhaven and Acushnet alone the style in vogue in the
Plymouth Colony.

Philip's War fell with devastating completeness on this
community and all dwellings in Dartmouth were destroyed
at the outset. Of the houses erected in the period immediately following this catastrophe, we have already described
one of the few remaining specimens in the Waite-Potter
house of Westport, built in 1677. This house, it will be
remembered, is of the primitive, end chimney type, common
to the early Rhode Island settlements.

In the eastern communities the use of the gambrel roof
followed the fashion of Plymouth and became the prevailing
style in the first quarter of the XVIIIth century.

The Summerton house of Acushnet, built in 1711, exhibits the familiar type of one and one half story, single chimney gambrel, similar to the William Harlow house of Plymouth and is the oldest gambrel-roofed house in this part of Massachusetts. The house fronts east, facing the hill on which

The Summerton House. New Bedford, Mass.

the first Meeting House was built. It has the characteristic features of overhanging cornice, massive chimney, and windows irregular in size and location, common to Plymouth houses of the period.

The Rev. Samuel Hunt, the young minister, married Hannah, the daughter of Captain Seth Pope, the wealthiest Puritan of the district and it is understood that the house was built for the young couple in the style which was considered at that time the most modern type of home. The homestead was used as a post office at one time and some of the cupboards and boxes still remain in the present kitchen. The fireplaces have been filled in and the framing timbers

The Hetty Green House.   New Bedford, Mass.

buried under lath and plaster so that but few internal evidences of its early history remain.

The Mrs. Hetty Green house on the Round Hill Farm, Dartmouth, combines the gambrel roof of the first quarter of the XVIIIth century with the square two and one half story central-chimney house of about seventy years later.

In 1695, John Russell conveyed an indefinite tract of land

including this property to Benjamin Howland. At his death in 1727 his farm included the present Round Hill Farm and the territory east to Salters Point. It was in this year that his son Barnabas built the gambrel roof section of the house and Barnabas' son, Stephen Howland, followed with the square addition previous to 1800. In 1813 the property was inherited by Abbey S. Howland, mother of Mrs. Hetty Green, the well known stock operator, a part of whose estate it still remains. The broad acres on which the old house stands have now been converted into a park by Mrs. Green's son, Colonel E. H. R. Green, extending to the Dumpling Light and to the point on which the present stone mansion stands. Near the house at the water's edge, a whaling bark, home from the seas but still with full sailing equipment aboard is held forever fixed in concrete to point the moral of the ancient mariner who guards her and to teach those born in a day of aeroplanes and ocean liners the true glories of the hardy adventurers who sailed the seven seas and brought back, not only the casks of oily wealth but the rough fibered courage and knowledge of the seas which have laid the foundations of our navy and our merchant marine.

The Henry Tucker homestead, of old Dartmouth, built in 1720, is of the second period among those houses which followed the Rhode Island tradition. The chimney and entrance are at one end, though the chimney is not built in the wall, the shape, a narrow oblong, two and one half stories in height without overhangs and without lean-to. It is one of the few Dartmouth farm houses of the early period remaining. Next to it is a larger house, now occupied by the present owners, which was built in 1809.

Henry Tucker was the founder of the Dartmouth Meeting of Friends. He owned extensive farms on the east side of Paskamansett River of which this is one. The Tucker Road named for him extended through them. An earlier house of stone, which was destroyed in Philip's War is believed to have been built on the same site. The present owner, Mr. Job

The Henry Tucker House.   New Bedford, Mass.

S. Gidley, married a daughter of Mr. Jesse Tucker, a descendant of the original Henry Tucker and the homestead has therefore remained in the same family since its establishment. Membership with the Friends has been continued and Mr. Gidley, though ninety years of age, still preaches at the Meeting House near by, each Sunday.

This older homestead faces south and looks into the garden of the later house which stands at right angles to it. Its interior has been much modernized but its summers and posts, now paneled, remain to mark its early origin.

The Morton-Almy mansion on the New Bedford Road, Westport, illustrates the third period of the west towns

The Morton-Almy House.   New Bedford, Mass.

development, late in the XVIIIth century when the houses of two stories were more elegant and larger though still simple and free from classical ornamentation as compared with contemporary building elsewhere in Massachusetts.

This house faces north. The western (right hand) end is the older construction and is believed to have been built by Peleg White, about the year 1800, while the eastern end was added by a later owner named Morton arout 1838. The land is part of a farm homestead granted to Nicholas Howland in 1710. The original chimney (west) is wholly or partly of stone. In the western end the corner posts are prominent but no other internal evidences of age remain, except

The Fairhaven Academy.   New Bedford, Mass.

the bricked up fireplaces corresponding with each chimney. There is a tradition that the house was at one time used as an inn. The three entrances lend color to this theory.

Turning from the Quaker to the Puritan settlement, the Fairhaven Academy, of about the same period as the Morton-Almy house, exhibits somewhat more the influence of the English classic style. This building has been moved from its original location and now stands on land belonging to the town of Fairhaven. It was built about 1795, before the day of public schools, and was intended to afford a more advanced education than was possible with the system of teaching then in vogue which provided no school houses and held its classes in private houses. The school rooms are left as they were originally with seats and desks of boards and a fireplace in each room as the only means of heating. On the second floor is a hall which was used for town meetings and was the central meeting place for both Acushnet and Fairhaven before they were separated. The first meetings of the Unitarian Society were held here. The building is now owned and occupied by the Fairhaven Historical Society.

New Bedford in the period of building following the one just illustrated erected several massive stone mansions, in the style called the American classic. One of these is described in a later chapter, thus completing the cycle of the town's architectural history.

William Penn, already converted to the Quaker faith, sent George Fox to long Island in 1672 believing that there he would find a promising field in the more liberal Puritan stock which had migrated from Massachusetts and New Haven to Dutch territory to escape the rigors of the Theocracy. Under two massive oaks whose location on Bowne Ave, Flushing is now marked by a rough boulder of granite, he preached the doctrine of the "Inward Light" that "at all times and in all places the human soul may be enlightened by direct communion with its Heavenly Father." He stripped from religion and from the relation between man and his Creator the non-essentials of doctrine and ritual

The Bowne House (West Front). Flushing, Long Island.

and taught the separation of Church and State, that the responsibility of the individual conscience to its God should not be hampered or abridged by intervening doctrine or clergy.

Across the road from the venerable oaks under which he preached stood the homestead of John Bowne, a well-to-do tradesman of Flushing, and it was to this house that he re-

The Bowne House (South Front). Flushing, Long Island.

tired when he had completed his discourse. In the corner of the present dining room, the old "Hall," may be seen the couch on which he rested after his labors.

Flushing was settled in 1645 by Puritan planters who had already lived in Holland and had imbibed tolerance in that religious oasis of Europe. John Bowne, from Mallock, Derbyshire, was one of George Fox's first converts and an enthusiast for the cause of the Friends. His home which had been built in 1661 was opened for their meetings but was soon reported to the Magistrates as a "Dangerous conventicle." Bowne was fined twenty-five pounds which he refused to pay and so he was imprisoned at Fort Amsterdam for three months, "For the welfare of the Community and to crush out as far as possible that abominable sect." His imprisonment made no change in his convictions; at the end of it he was as "obdurate" as at the beginning; continuing so, he was remanded to the States General in Holland by the good ship *Gilded Fox* and on his arrival there at once laid his case before the West India Company. He was immediately released but remained to plead the cause of the long suffering sect who in the Dutch phraseology were "in skorne called Quakers." Two years later he returned to Flushing a warmer friend than ever of the Friends, to find that most of the inhabitants of the village, in spite of persecution, had followed him in joining the "Dangerous conventicle."

The overzealousness of Peter Stuyvesant (for what he had felt to be his duty) was summarily rebuked by the West India Company: "Let everyone remain free as long as he is modest, moderate and his political conduct irreproachable and he does not offend others or the Government."

For a generation after John Bowne's return, his house served as a Friends' Meeting House, the meetings being held in the "Hall," now used as dining room. In 1696 the present Meeting House was built around the corner from the Bowne house and has continued to perform its function practically unchanged to the present day.

The old homestead was originally a single chimney, two

and a half story house of the Massachusetts and Connecticut type with a lean-to and it is only within the last generation that the rear roof has been raised to provide additional room for the family. The ell shown in the illustration of the east front is nearly, if not quite, as old as the original building. This ell has its own chimney with a very large fireplace, perhaps a ten- or twelve-foot opening, and here during the major part of its existence the cooking has been done. To provide a back log for the fire a tree of moderate size was cut to the required length and the log hauled to the kitchen by horse power. As doors front and back opposite each other were provided, the horse was driven in one door and out the other leaving the back log to be rolled by hand behind the spit. The two main living rooms flank the main entrance to the right and the left. The door, in the Dutch fashion, is cut in two in the middle. The typical Massachusetts stairway against the chimney has two plain rails, one over the other, without spindles. The "Hall" to the right is the chamber used for the Friends' Meetings. It is paneled throughout with framing exposed including corner posts and a floor of broad planks. The fireplace in this room is the next in size to that of the kitchen. The "Parlor" at the left, has excellent paneling around the fireplace. One of its posts carries the large bracket so often referred to as a "ship's knee." In this room is a very handsome highboy of the early XVIIIth century which was entirely constructed in the room by the cabinet maker. This plan of building a piece of furniture in the room it is intended to furnish was not uncommon during the period of small doors and windows. Back of the parlor is a bedroom furnished in every detail in XVIIIth century style.

This is divided from another small room back of the "Hall" by a hallway and back entrance, these two rooms and hall taking the place of the original lean-to chamber.

The Bowne house was, until 1804, the home of successive John Bownes; since then it has continued the homestead of the same family on the mother's side now represented by the tenth generation.

In this house we have an excellently preserved New England homestead of the XVIIth century, which has been continuously occupied by the same family of pure English stock, located within the limits of Greater New York, an interesting example of the persistence of the characteristic building which expressed the English inheritance in spite of local influence to the contrary.

Nantucket, much more than New Bedford, has adapted the New England homestead to a distinct type of building all its own, more or less uniform and distinguished by a marked flavor of its seafaring life.

The settlers of Nantucket left Massachusetts Bay for their new home in June, 1661, bringing with them their cattle and belongings. These first emigrants were not poor and they found in their new home broad acres occupied by a handful only of Indians who welcomed them, and an abundance of fish. It is doubtful if the Island ever produced timber in sufficient quantities for building and in all probability building material was transported by the first comers. It is of record that Nathaniel Barnard imported pine from Merrimack in 1670. Rhode Island stones were used for chimneys before 1700 and clay beds were opened on the Island in 1720. The first carpenter, John Bishop, came from the Merrimack valley and the earliest houses, therefore,

follow Newbury. (See Tristram Coffin house, Chapter
V.) The removal of the town from Wacunacomet, about
two miles down the shore from its present location to the
inner bay called Wiscoe, took place in 1720. A few houses
had been built in the new location in 1680 but most of them

The Major Josiah Coffin House. Nantucket.

after 1720. It is not safe therefore to credit any Nantucket
house with greater age than this indicates unless it is supported by convincing evidence. One well authenticated
exception is the Jethro Coffin or Horse Shoe House, built in
1686, described in Chapter II.

The Major Josiah Coffin house is marked 1689, that is,
three years later than the Jethro Coffin house. It is a two

story lean-to and the natural evolution of the Jethro Coffin house which is a one-story lean-to. If the date given is correct it is the second oldest house on the Island. A writer for the *Bulletin* of the Nantucket Historical Society, however, believes it among those houses built after the town was moved to its present location, which would place the date around 1720. With its full second story and kitchen in the lean-to, it is much more of a house than the Jethro Coffin cottage and is the best specimen of the old type on the Island. The walls are covered with shingles rather than clapboards as are all the old Nantucket houses and the central chimney is the dominant feature. It is as plain and unadorned as a house could very well be. As in the case of many Nantucket houses, the front door is not exactly in the middle but is placed where the builder preferred to have it. This makes the "Hall" somewhat larger than the "Parlor." This room has some good paneling about the fireplace and both hall and parlor and the chambers above show summers and corner posts. The stairway still runs up against the chimney but has been somewhat widened to satisfy modern ideas of comfort. The chimney has been repaired but is original.

The early Nantucket families intermarried to such an extent that each one is related to all the others and many of the familiar names are mentioned in connection with every house. This house passed to Major Josiah Coffin for whom it is named and his granddaughter married Benjamin Gardner, popularly known as Squire Ben Gardner. His daughter, Mrs. Eunice Coffin Brooks, was the owner in 1906. In addition to these families, the house has sheltered Folgers and for the longest period a branch of the Macy clan of which family the present owner is a descendant.

Many of the oldest houses in type and appearance though not actually so in point of age are found across the Island on the exposed shore at the village of Siasconset.

'Sconset was originally a hamlet of fishermen's huts. Most of the oldest cottages were first built at a point two and a half miles north of the present location at Sesachacha (Sachacha for short) the other side of Sankaty Head and were taken down and moved on carts to the present village.

The 'Sconset house was at first a one room hut with a wooden chimney, most of the village dating from about the time of the Revolution. They were at first used by men alone as shelters merely during the fishing season but as the women folk found them pleasant and amusing to visit, they were expanded to accommodate families. The wooden chimneys were replaced with stone and floors were laid. For the clinker built roof, shingles were substituted. Windows were added, of varying sizes to be sure, and doors which swing out, hung on wooden hinges and gudgeons and fastened with wooden buttons and latches. At one end of the single room an extension was added, a lean-to. These extensions were called "warts" and were often not over seven feet square, but large enough for a bed. Often a second story was added to the wart three to four feet in height with a small opening into the main room reached by cleats nailed to the wall. The boys were stowed away in cots slung in these tiny attics. At the other end of the main room was often added another extension called the "porch." This was also a lean-to and was used as a kitchen. Most 'Sconset houses have been moved several times. It is truly a town of shreds and patches, so slight and ethereal the tiny cottages seem;

they appear to the visitor the figments of a dream rather than dwellings in reality.

Many of the cottages are built of odds and ends, the jetsam of wrecks, the timbers and planks used are often out of all proportion to the size of the cottage and the brick

"*Auld Lang Syne.*" '*Sconset, Mass.*

chimneys which have now replaced the early wooden affairs likewise are often disproportioned to the buildings they serve. Actually, however, a kind of architecture has been developed.

As whaling became important, 'Sconset grew to be the resort of Nantucketers. Inns were built and the village started on its career as a place of amusement and relaxation. Here the young sailor brought his sweetheart in a buggy or his family in a "surrey." Its peak of prosperity was reached in 1845 when it boasted about sixty homes.

Prosperity left 'Sconset as well as Nantucket when whaling became unprofitable and for a generation the village, reduced to a hamlet, fell into a state of innocuous desuetude.

George C. Gardner House. 'Sconset, Mass.

The cottage "Auld Lang Syne" is beyond question the oldest on the Bank. The date claimed for it is 1675, that is, long before the Town existed on its present site. The earliest owner was Micah Coffin who employed Indians to fish for him during the season while he remained ashore and did the cooking. He was the great-grandfather of Captain Edward C. Joy, well known to later generations. At the chimney

end, the cottage has a large fireplace with chimney piece
exposed and the room is open to the roof. Over the other
end is one of the minature garrets already described, reached
by cleats in the wall. The cottage is apparently unchanged

The Abel Gardner House. Nantucket, Mass.

from its original design and its sagging floors and rafters
testify to its age.

The George C. Gardner house, built by Prince Gardner in
1814, is larger than most 'Sconset houses. With its roof
sloping equally on both sides and its Beverly ell, it seems a
small edition of a Cape Cod house except that the chimney
is at the end and not in the middle. It is now the property
of the Nantucket Historical Society and is used as the Public Library of 'Sconset.

Turning back to Nantucket we find another of the old families represented in the Abel Gardner house built in 1733. This substantial cottage with its two entrances oddly located and its sturdy plastered brick chimney was originally a

The Grindell Gardner House. Nantucket, Mass.

one room house in width with the chimney at the end. The west room (left end) was added first and the lean-to finally completed the cottage as it now stands. The two front rooms still have the summers and corner posts with ship's knees exposed.

Across the road is the Grindell Gardner house built by Abel Gardner for his son in 1772. This cottage has the typical gambrel roof with overhang on the front combined with an ordinary peak roof in the rear. To complete the bizarre effect the favorite jut-out or Beverly ell is added to the rear.

The Ray house, the date of whose construction is given as antedating 1745, originally a square central chimney, two and a half story house has as a later addition, an ell with a

The Ray House. Nantucket, Mass.

comfortable lean-to of its own and its own chimney. The builder has shown excellent judgment in choosing the point at which the two buildings are joined. The marriage of the two with its foreground of garden is certainly a happy one and the resulting ensemble is one of the most charming in the Town.

The interior of the older part has very fine plain paneling, floors of wide planking and narrow entry while the fireplace in the rear room has a double decked oven at the side, of curious construction.

One of the most characteristic of the early XVIIIth century ship master's houses is the homestead of Captain Joshua Coffin, built in 1756 or earlier. The oldest part was originally built at Sherburne, a nearby village, and moved to its present location. This, the front section in the illustration, was as now, a square two and one half story gable-roofed house. After it was moved in 1756, the adjoining ell with its chimney was added and lastly the woodshed, in the shape of a lean-to, completed the three generations of the building.

Previous to the Revolution a section was taken out of the front of the chimney to allow for a capacious storeroom which Captain Coffin designed as a concealed safe deposit for his valuables in the event of an anticipated British raid on the Island. The steep narrow stairway rises, as usual, apparently against the chimney stack and the presence of the storeroom would not be suspected if it were not for a window which has now been let into the front wall on the second floor which discloses the inner stairway running from the cellar to the attic terminating at a trap concealed in the attic floor. The usual fireplaces on both floors remain, with seven flues running to the one chimney. The house is built over a very high cellar which is paved with cobble stones. These stones are the product of the surrounding fields and have formed from the earliest period the raw material of Nantucket's street paving wherever paving has been adopted.

The bedrooms are paneled about the fireplaces distinctly

The Captain Joshua Coffin House. Nantucket, Mass.

in the manner of a ship's cabin. The walk on the roof is easily reached by stairway from the attic, demonstrating its convenience and frequent use, and furnishes an extended view of the harbor and Town—a sea of sloping, shingled roofs and fat chimneys interspersed with trees with a border of blue sky and water.

All the men of this family from Captain Joshua down have followed the sea, with the exception of the present representative. He was the only son left after the loss of his elder brother in the navy near the end of the Civil War and was withheld from following his inclinations by the strongly expressed wish of his parents. His father, Captain Henry F. Coffin, shipped on the whaler *Ploughboy*, of which his father was part owner for a five year cruise when he was thirteen years of age and he bore the mark of this voyage to his dying day. The souvenir of his narrow escape was a scar on his leg made by a splinter from the whale boat in which he was serving which was crushed by the jaws of a whale. On this occasion all the ship's boats were following the spouting monsters and at the time of the accident the nearest boat was four miles away and the ship itself still further. The men clung to the spars and rigging all night, young Henry sharing an oar with the first mate. In the morning the ship came on them but swung about so suddenly that to save themselves they were compelled to dive under the keel and come up at her stern. All were saved from the sea, but one of the sailors subsequently died from wounds.

In the attic, record remains, in chalk on the beams, of sundry voyages, including the names of many famous whalers of which the Coffins were masters and part owners, such as the *Ploughboy* of 1827, the *Lima* of 1828, the *Rose* of 1829, the *Swift*, *Lopez* and *Conqueror* of later dates.

Henry Coffin, in spare moments in the forecastle and later, as a petty officer, educated himself by the light of his sperm oil lamp so successfully that when he came to take his examination in New York he was given an A.A. rating as both Pilot and Ship's master at the first trial.

Nantucket produced men of such caliber as this, inured to hardship and keen for knowledge and of the fiber from which a strong race is bred.

At the height of its prosperity, between 1830 and 1840, Nantucket in spite of its Quaker leanings yielded to the urge of the times and its ship owners built mansions more elegant in design, following Georgian traditions, yet still marked with the island's characteristic touch. Three of these houses are included in a later chapter.

The only remaining Meeting House of the Friends is now a part of the museum of the Nantucket Historical Society. Its presence is a reminder that the doctrine of the Inward Light prevailed during the greater part of Nantucket's history and is doubtless responsible for the harmonious simplicity of the Town's general plan and of its architecture.

The charm of Nantucket is perennial; it does not grow less with the years. The writer remembers William Clark, the last town crier, who rang his bell every morning on the main corners to announce the temperatures of New York, Philadelphia and Chicago, that sojourners might be duly grateful that they were in Nantucket. This simple method of disseminating the news persisted to the present generation and is typical of many things about the old Town.

In spite of the presence of fifteen hundred automobiles

on the island, one can still renew the past by a ride in one of Nantucket's "surreys." The Island cannot be adequately seen or felt from a car. Up and down the narrow lanes on foot if one is to imbibe the salt sea life, a view of the Bay and the Town from one of the "walks" and an amble across the downs in a surrey behind old Dobbin, will put one in the mood to acquire the feeling of Nantucket's remoteness, her ancient flavor, her indefinable charm, the essence of all her qualities. Once gained, it will never be lost but will return with each recurring spring to draw the cave dweller of the cities once more to the wide freedom of her spacious atmosphere.

CHAPTER VIII

THE REVOLUTION.   POST ROAD TAVERNS

FROM our present point of vantage it can readily be shown that the divergence between the colonies and the mother country began soon after the landing of the Pilgrims on these shores, and was the natural, perhaps the inevitable, result of the conditions which brought about the migration, coupled with the difference in development which took place on the two sides of the Atlantic.   The distance which separated the planters from their official rulers weakened their sense of dependence on the central power and made them of necessity self-dependent and from self-dependence it was but a natural step to independence. And thus, in 1643, only seven years after the establishment of Connecticut, the four New England colonies formed a Confederation for their mutual protection, a protection which the remote government at home could not furnish.

At this time and for a hundred years thereafter a voyage across the Atlantic was a perilous undertaking.   From seven weeks to six months were required for the transit, the vessels were small and the space allotted to each passenger contracted and the conditions to which emigrants, even those of wealth and position, were forced to submit were, to our modern notions, unbelievably bad.   These difficulties reduced the number of emigrants to those inspired by very strong reasons for changing their habitat and by the same token when they had accomplished in safety the voyage and had survived the establishment of their families in the new world, they gained a sense of achievement which bred an independence of spirit and brooked no interference from those who had not been chastened by a like ordeal. And so from the very first their development grew of itself from the foundation of English liberties which they had brought with them, unburdened with the traditions of life in Europe which they had left behind.

Within a generation, the people assembled in the Old South Meeting House, Boston, refused to surrender the charter of Massachusetts Bay and when it was annulled by arbitrary enactment without their consent, they protested through John Wise of Ipswich against the payment of taxes levied under the Royal Charter by the King's agent. These measures were not seriously oppressive in themselves but were the evidences of interference by a power already recognized as alien by the colonists. Preparations were made by Massachusetts to resist by force the application of authority and a clash was imminent when the welcome news was received of the landing of the Prince of Orange on English shores. This event postponed for another generation the contest which grew more inevitable as the breach widened.

At the beginning of the XVIIIth century the New England colonies were considerably in advance of the homeland in political thinking. During the period ending with the accession of William, England had been occupied with the Revolution, the Commonwealth and the Restoration and intensely absorbed with its political problems at home had left the colonists to their own development. This succession of events gave the colonists, who in New England did not increase materially by emigration after 1640, nearly three quarters of a century to create and perfect their own political institutions. In New England there was no reaction to arbitrary rule such as that which resulted from the Restoration in England but a steady progress toward the greater freedom of the individual. This political concept was first definitely expressed in the written constitution of Connecticut which established a theory of government more advanced than political thought in England warranted.

At this time, therefore, the colonists were prepared to demand their full rights as Englishmen to all English liberties. After the accession of William and Mary all the colonies except Connecticut and Rhode Island, who elected their own governors, became royal provinces with governors appointed by the Crown, performing executive functions, limited however on the legislative side by popularly elected assemblies. In this relationship the governor stood as the representative of royal power and the assembly represented the people. The two were radically and continuously opposed, the latter seeking constantly to enlarge its powers and the former laboring equally to restrict them. The Assembly however held the purse strings and controlled the salaries of the governor and his assistants and this power the representatives of the people did not hesitate to use to their advantage.

Not only was the contest constantly in progress in each colony but the colonies possessed a strong sense of loyalty to each other as against the common enemy in the shape of the royal power. As early as 1754 a congress was held at Albany at which seven colonies were represented to discuss the need of greater unity. At this congress Benjamin Franklin proposed a self-sustaining Federal government of the colonies represented by a grand council of delegates from each. This plan was accepted by the congress but was not supported by the individual colonies.

While the colonies were seeking to knit their own relations more closely and to fortify themselves against aggression from overseas, the autocratic government of George the Third, mistakenly viewing the colonies as a legitimate field for exploitation, was searching a means of raising a revenue from them. The issue came in the Stamp Act of 1764, followed by the Townshend taxes on tea, oil, wine, glass, paper, etc.

Samuel Adams, Massachusetts agitator and shrewd political leader, was the first formally to deny the right of Parliament to tax the colonies without their consent. Five other colonies at once joined in Massachusetts' protest and a year later the Stamp Act Congress was held at which nine colonies were represented. All thirteen colonies were unanimous in opposition and it became clear that the law could not be enforced without a war. It was then that Pitt reminded the government in England that America was upholding the eternal principles dear to all Englishmen and said, "In such a cause your success would be hazardous. America if she fell would fall like the strong man with his arms around the pillars of the Constitution."

But Parliament was not then a body of free men. The House of Commons was controlled by a few old Whig families whose heads sat in the House of Lords and held the power of the Commons in their hands through the rotten borough system then in vogue. The aggressive minority under William Pitt and Edmund Burke, called the "New Whigs," were eventually to prevail but not until too late to save the colonies. George the Third, past master in political manipulation, used the Tories to destroy the old Whig families and to subdue the new Whigs. To hold the political control of England in the Crown it was absolutely necessary that the American ideal of political liberty should be abolished. In this sense King George was principally responsible for the Revolution and for him as well as for the colonies it was a desperate struggle for political existence. The measures which brought the final rupture would not have been considered tyrannical by a less developed people but were abhorrent to the colonists who had reached an advanced conception of political liberty.

These measures of King George's government fall into three stages in their development: the dispute over the Stamp Act, the attempts to raise revenue by taxation and, finally, coercive measures intended to force compliance with the royal will.

The Stamp Act was repealed but Parliament retained its right to make laws for the colonies in "all cases whatsoever," and within a year the direct issue was raised again in the Townshend taxes. This invited resistance and was at once met by a boycott against English goods on the part of the colonists.

Samuel Adams, the prophet of the Revolution, with a keener political insight than his fellows, declared as early as 1768 that the only course open to the colonies was to declare themselves independent of England, unite in a permanent confederation and invite European alliances. This position he maintained in the face of opposition, until it was generally accepted in 1776.

Coercion, once determined, its inevitable results in the conflict of brother against brother were made manifest without delay. England threw down the gauntlet and the colonies accepted the challenge but left it to the English levies to fire the first shot. Once blood was spilled complete subjugation of the rebellious provinces or independence were seen to be the only alternatives.

Boston's resistance to the taxes furnished the excuse for the quartering on her citizens of two regiments of English troops. The inevitable result followed in the Boston massacre of 1770. The shedding of blood aroused and united the citizens. The governor yielded to the storm of protest and the troops were withdrawn. The next attempt, that of the government to force cargoes of tea on the colonies, was met in Boston by the wholesale destruction at the Boston Tea Party of 1773.

Punitive measures followed, the charter of Massachusetts Bay was withdrawn and the Port of Boston closed to commerce, and again the capitol city became the headquarters for an English army with General Gage in command. The countryside armed, drilled and collected munitions and supplies but was determined to await the first blow from the royal troops. To meet General Gage's call for twenty thousand men the Congress of the thirteen colonies met at Philadelphia, September 5, 1774, and in Massachusetts the Provincial Congress with John Hancock as chairman assumed the government of the province outside of the city of Boston.

An attempt to seize stores collected at Salem in February, 1775, met with failure and finally on April 19 a battalion of four hundred infantry, augmented to eighteen hundred later in the day, was dispatched to Concord to seize the stores there, of which the British spy John How had given information. The countryside had been aroused by the midnight ride from Boston of Paul Revere and William Dawes and as the battalion of English regulars formed on Lexington Green they were opposed by Captain Parker and seventy-seven of his Minute men. Ordered to lay down their arms, they stood their ground. The order to fire was given and the Minute men whose blood watered the Green of their native village, became the first sacrifice to the cause of independence.

Just as in their political thinking the people of New England advanced along a line so divergent from that of the homeland that the breach between the two finally grew too wide to be bridged, so also in the architecture of their dwellings they developed in their own characteristic fashion, adapting traditions which they brought from and which came to them from over seas to the ideas of living which grew out of their six generations of experience in the new world.

Beginning with the typical cottage of East Anglia the New England dwelling grew through various stages, differing in the different localities, into the Georgian mansion of the Revolution. While there is variation among the Revolutionary houses arising from the conservatism or progressiveness of the communities which have produced them, perhaps the most typical is the oblong three story gambrel roofed house with chimney at each end which has yielded to Georgian tradition in its wide central hallway and its classic decorations.

In Lexington, however, the tendency was toward the square hip roof similar to houses of Portsmouth and the Maine coast.

The Jonathan Harrington, Jr., house faces Lexington Battle Green about a hundred feet behind the line at which the Minute men stood their ground and received the fire of the British Grenadiers. Harrington, one of the seventy-seven, was shot, but dragged himself to the doorstep of this house

The Harrington House. Lexington, Mass.

and died there at his wife's feet. The date at which the house was built is not known but it was probably not earlier than 1750. It was restored and embellished in 1910.

Captain Parker and his small band were no match for the four hundred Grenadiers opposed to them. After losing eight of their number in killed and nine wounded they fell back and the enemy, whose numbers were now increased to twelve hundred by the arrival of Colonel Smith with a regiment of regulars, advanced towards their objective at Concord. The British divided into reconnoitering parties were now harassed by Minute men coming up from near-by towns. The militia was sufficiently strengthened by fresh arrivals to meet the main body of British and repulse it in the second engagement, which was at the old North Bridge in Concord. This skirmish marked the farthest advance of the enemy. The order was here given to retreat and Col. Smith's troops fell back on Lexington where they met the reinforcements sent by General Gage under Earl Percy and the whole detachment, after a delay to reform and rest, marched back to Charlestown harassed and depleted on the way by the rising countryside, now grown to a formidable army.

The Old Manse stands but a stone's throw from the North Bridge in Concord. The Rev. William Emerson, then pastor of the Concord church, was married in 1766, after Lecture, and three years later he built this house for his bride. Mrs. Emerson sat in her bedroom on the second floor and viewed the fight at the Bridge and not without misgivings did she see the British retire before the New England yeomanry, since her own family was divided in sentiment, some of its members holding still to the older order and others espousing the cause of the patriots. Her husband, however, became a chaplain of the Revolutionary army, was taken ill at Ticonderoga and died in the service. His successor, the Rev. Ezra Ripley, took up his residence with Mrs. Emerson at the Manse and four years later they were married. The congregation made objection to the marriage on account of Mr. Ripley's age and also because of his residence in the same house. Mr. Ripley intimated

The Old Manse. Concord, Mass.

that he would relinquish his heart's desire, but warned the committee that if he did so a like restraint would be expected of all other members and that thereafter the congregation must reconcile itself to celibacy. After prayerful consideration the congregation withdrew its objection, and for sixty years he preached in Concord and died there in the odor of sanctity at the ripe old age of ninety years. The property was divided between the Emerson and the Ripley children by a roadway which runs through it and the homestead is now owned and occupied by the fourth generation of Ripleys.

Ralph Waldo Emerson was a grandson of the Rev. William Emerson but lived in his own house on the Lexington Road. Nathaniel and Mrs. Hawthorne lived in this house from 1843–46 and here he wrote "Mosses from an Old Manse." The Hawthornes, as witness to the charm of the old mansion, have left a verse, scratched on a window pane of the west bedroom. In the old attic bedroom, as well, several generations of Emersons have recorded their presence in pencil on the door frame.

With the exception of two additions the house stands today as it was built in 1769. The dormer was cut in 1846 and the small bow window added in 1875.

Its narrow, oblong shape and gambrel roof with long lean-to form a combination unusual in the Revolutionary period and manifest the conservatism of its builder who held to the ancient tradition of the lean-to while yielding to the fashion of the times in other respects. The end chimneys permit the spaciousness of the interior plan which is gained by the central hall running from front to rear flanked by the large square chambers, each with its ample fireplace.

The stairs are broad with low risers and the hallway is paneled half way in dark wood. There is paneling also in the parlor and living room.

The interior of this old house is like its exterior, simple and dignified, and expresses in its warm hospitality the cultured and generous living of its six generations.

The town Taverns or Ordinaries played a very important part in the Revolution. For a generation men had found the news of the day in these Inns. In them they had met their fellows and discussed business and politics. Many public meetings were held in the Tavern rather than in the Meeting House. In 1768 an association of the New England yeomanry was formed which held its meetings in the Public Houses. It was named the "Sons of Liberty." Landlords began to dedicate the elms which shaded their hostelries as "Liberty Trees" and soon every town had a "Liberty Tree" or "Liberty Pole." On many occasions, when the weather was favorable, meetings of the Sons of Liberty were held under these trees. James Otis and Samuel Adams fostered these associations as they kept alive the spirit of patriotism and informed the countryside of the progress of the dispute with Great Britain. John Adams also often spoke at their meetings. These reunions and the idea which they represented became so popular that before long mine host let it be known, often by a line on his sign board that "herein might be found entertainment for the 'Sons of Liberty'." A new Liberty Song became the vogue. The Committees of Safety held their meetings in the Taverns and they were often the repositories for the town arms. After the fighting had begun the taprooms became the headquarters of recruiting officers.

The night of April 18, 1775, after the session of the Committee of Safety and Supplies at Witherby's Black Horse Tavern between Cambridge and Lexington, Hancock and Adams left for Lexington where they spent the night with the Rev. Jonas Clarke. The Marblehead members of the Committee, Messrs. Orne, Lee and Gerry remained for the night at Witherby's. During the evening they saw English officers and men on the high road and forwarded this information to Hancock and Adams at Lexington. They went to bed, however, not expecting to be disturbed but were awakened at midnight and informed that a body of British troops were close at hand and approaching the Tavern. The three patriots threw on such clothes as were available and concealed themselves in a nearby field and thus escaped capture. This was the battalion under Major Pitcairn which encountered the first rally of Minute men on Lexington Green a few hours later. Witherby's Inn was destroyed a few years ago.

The Minute men, aroused by the message of Revere and Dawes, were assembled in the taproom of the Buckman Tavern at Lexington which faces the Green on the east about opposite the line established by the British infantry on their arrival.

Solomon Brown, one of the Minute men, met the advance guard of the British approaching Lexington during the night and was captured by them as was also Paul Revere. Brown was released, however, near the Buckman Tavern and took up his post at the rear door of the Inn. From this point he fired on the British line and the latter returned the fire. He then passed through to the front door and fired again. During this encounter Brown was not struck but several British bullets buried themselves in the walls of the Inn. There they may still be seen as witnesses to the intimate connection of this old hostelry with the first battle of the Revolution.

The Buckman Tavern, built by Benjamin Muzzey in 1690, is the oldest of Lexington inns. Its landlord in 1775

The Buckman Tavern. Lexington, Mass.

was John Buckman a member of Captain Parker's Company. It was at this period the Tavern for carriage folk, in contrast to many of the Ordinaries of the time which were the common resort of farmers when traveling with their produce to and from market.

The building, of the square hip roof type, remains in

its exterior practically as it was the day of the battle. The interior is being restored to its original condition by the removal of plaster and paper. In removing several layers of paint from the wall of the taproom, a line showing the original level of the bar was disclosed and the bar itself, which was found in the cellar, has been restored to its original location. The taproom thus restored, with its large fireplace, summer beam, joists and girths furnished with settle, chairs and table of the period, offers us an excellent picture of the village taproom of the Revolution, the scene of so many dramatic episodes, the rallying point during the long years of discouragement and the center finally in which victory was celebrated and the surviving heroes of Washington's army welcomed back to their peaceful countryside.

It is fitting that the old Inn should become the property of the Town as it has and that it should have been used during the World War as the center of the Town's local war activities.

When Earl Percy reached Lexington during the afternoon of the 19th, with reinforcements, he made his headquarters in the Munroe Tavern located about a mile east of the green on the Boston Post Road. Here his wounded received attention and it was at this point that juncture was made with the battalions of Col. Smith and Maj. Pitcairn and the whole force reformed for the retreat on Charlestown. To protect the movement, he planted a cannon in the road and bombarded the Meeting House and Green, and another on the hill above the Tavern. During the halt, houses and barns were burned and the cripple, Raymond, left in charge of the Inn by Sergeant Munroe, the landlord, was killed.

The delay at the Tavern gave the farmers time to come up and line the high road to Charlestown so that the British battalions were harassed by a force probably twice their number, well protected by stone walls and other obstacles familiar to them. The day ended, therefore, in the complete

The Munroe Tavern. Lexington, Mass.

failure of the British objective and a loss in killed and wounded considerably larger than that of the Continentals.

The Munroe Tavern was built in 1695 by William Munroe. His grandson, Sergeant William Munroe, the proprietor in 1775, was fighting with Captain Parker's Company when the Inn was occupied, while his wife and children were hidden in the woods behind the house. The house has been modernized to some extent but retains much of its ancient flavor and shelters many historical relics of interest and value. The shallow entry with its narrow stairs remains and the public room has some good paneling around the fireplace. Summers and girths in the rooms on both floors are in evidence but encased. Through bequest of the last owner it has become the property of the Lexington Historical Society.

In the period just antedating the Revolution this Tavern was the rendezvous of the drovers on their way to market. The most picturesque but the most difficult to handle of their livestock were the turkeys, due to their inveterate habit of roosting at nightfall wherever they might be. The trees about the Inn were filled of an autumn night with the roosting birds and in the early dawn the procession reformed with the gobblers in the van and the herdsmen bringing up the rear.

The Inn catered at one time to a more fashionable element, as shown by the ell which was added during the Revolutionary period containing a ballroom twenty by sixty which was used as a center for social functions. This addition has been removed.

Washington spent the day at Lexington November 5, 1789, during his tour of New England when returning from New Hampshire, and dined at the Tavern. On his arrival he viewed the battle Green and the Buckman Tavern and talked with the survivors of the fight. Sergeant Munroe received him at the Munroe Tavern and served him dinner in the Parlor chamber in which the hatrack, table, chair and dishes which he used may still be seen.

Washington talks much in his diary about the Inns on

this trip and marks some as good and some as bad. The absence of class distinctions impresses him; he finds but few or no "opulent men" and no poor.[1] He speaks also of the great similitude of the buildings "the general fashion of which is a chimney (always of stone or brick) and a door in the middle with a staircase fronting the latter . . . two flush stories with a very good show of sash and glass windows. The size generally is from thirty to fifty feet in length and from twenty to thirty feet in width, exclusive of a back shed, which seems to be added as the family increased." He traveled at the rate of thirty miles or more in a day by "wheels and carriage." This is in contrast to that earlier journey over part of the same route which has come down to us in the journal of Madam Sarah Kemble Knight. Madam Knight made the trip on horseback alone, an extraordinary feat for a woman at that time, in 1704, from Boston to New York and returned by practically the same route. The time required was two weeks each way and the obstacles, such as the fording of turbulent streams and the scarcity of Inns on the route as well as the deficiences of their service, recounted in a humorous vein have preserved for us an amusing picture of travel in that primitive time. It was not until 1784 that a regular stage was run between Boston, Hartford and New York (by Captain Levi Pease, called the father of the turnpike). The time required for the journey by stage to New York was one week. In 1786 a line of stages ran from Portsmouth, New Hampshire, to Savannah, Georgia, to carry mail and passengers, the rate charged the latter being three pence per mile.

[1] "Diaries of George Washington," edited by Joseph A. Hoskins, Summerfield, N. C., 1921.

The Wright Tavern, Concord, built in 1747, always used as a Public House, was the headquarters of Major Pitcairn after the battle of Lexington and had been the rallying point for the Concord Minute men before the fight.   Captain

The Wright Tavern.   Concord, Mass.

Smith and his company from Lincoln also reported here. The house was opened as an Ordinary in 1747 by a militia captain named Ephraim Jones and was deeded to Thomas Munroe in 1751 and to Amos Wright in 1775.

The cellar of the Inn was originally used as a village bake house and has still the huge fireplace and brick oven designed for this purpose.   The taproom was on the ground floor. The building is original as it stands excepting the north ell which has been added within the last twenty-five years. The roof has been renewed. The building followed the Lexington-Concord fashion and is square in shape, with two and one-half stories, and hip roof with four chimneys.

The Shipman or Hunters Tavern.   Rocky Hill, Conn.

The Shipman or Hunters Tavern of Rocky Hill, Connecticut, built in 1770, is a different type of Revolutionary Ordinary adapted to the Connecticut style of building.

Rocky Hill, originally called Stepney or Stepney Landing, was a parish of Wethersfield and from its landing a ferry in the old days ran across the Connecticut to South Glastonbury. In size and in point of business activity Stepney Landing was a much more important town at the time of the Revolution than at present is Rocky Hill, a suburb of Hartford. For the last forty years before it was separated, this section of Wethersfield was called "Shipman's Hill" from the location of this Inn at its foot which was for many years kept by Mr., generally called "Uncle," Sam Shipman.

Through the open doorway of the eastern ell can be seen the narrow stair rising against the chimney which shows this to be the original section built undoubtedly as a central chimney two and one half story house. The piazza is of course a modern innovation. The Palladian window of the west ell lights a ballroom, a very frequent addition to the Inns of the period. The original section was built by Captain Wait Robbins. Samuel Ball was the landlord until 1800 and he was followed by Simeon Williams, who built the ell containing the ballroom. Others intervened and the Inn closed its history as an Ordinary with the death of Sam Shipman in 1875. In Shipman's time there was a nine-pin alley and the old house became a famous resort for Hartford people as Mrs. Shipman was famous for her cooking, particularly for shad in season. The ballroom was often used by sleighing parties.

One of the main roads out of Boston in the XVIIIth century was the north shore road to Portsmouth and this road became the route of the first stage coach running north and south.

The Ross Tavern, located on this road in the village of Ipswich, had an importance in that day which it does not now possess as it stood at the main crossing of the Ipswich River. A cart bridge existed at this point as early as 1648. In 1764 the old bridge was found too narrow by six or eight feet for

the increased travel and a new bridge twenty feet wide was
planned by the town. The present stone bridge was finally
built at a cost of approximately one thousand pounds. Col.
John Choate, judge of the Court of General Sessions managed
the undertaking and carried it to a successful conclusion, at

The Ross Tavern. Ipswich, Mass.

the behest of the Board of Selectmen and it has been known
since as the Choate Bridge and is the oldest stone bridge on
the continent.

The Tavern is built on the part of the Appleton property
which abutted the bridge on the south and was sold to
Thomas Buckman, Jr., in 1736 after several transfers. This
is the first mention of a house on this spot and it is believed

that the earliest section of the house was built about 1734. After several succeeding transfers the house and lot were deeded to Jeremiah Ross in 1809. Ross maintained the Inn and it has since been known as the Ross Tavern.

The present owner, Mr. Ralph W. Burnham, who is restoring the house so far as possible to its original condition, believes that the south front (right end) facing the road, which then undoubtedly passed in front of it, is the oldest, the middle section the next and the north end on the river the most recent. It is an interesting fact that the old south building was originally built with a large framed overhang about sixteen inches deep on the south and west side at the second story, the upper floors being supported by girths worked to an O. G. molding. The molding and all the details of the original construction are plainly visible on the inside now but were obliterated to the public view, by extending the second story clapboards to the foundation when the fashion for overhangs departed. Mr. Burnham is removing the later accretion and will eventually show the old building as originally constructed. The several additions to the first building are made apparent inside by the many different levels on both floors, the hallways leading to the present twenty-two rooms rambling amiably in every direction. The main rooms of the old building show the original summers on both floors. The lower entrance stairway has been restored but the stair to the attic is original, dividing half way up into two sections on each side of the chimney. The chimney itself is original with the usual large fireplaces.

We have next to consider the most famous of old New England Taverns, the Wayside Inn of Sudbury, built by David How in 1683 and opened as the How Tavern in 1686.

David was the grandson of John How, who was a tavern keeper in 1661, prominent in the church and a selectman. For four generations thereafter, including David, a How officiated as mine host. At the time of the Revolution Colonel Ezekiel How, the inn keeper, was an important man

The Wayside Inn. Sudbury, Mass.

in the community. In 1775 he was Lieut. Col. of the 4th Regiment of the Middlesex County militia of which James Barrett of Concord was Colonel, and in 1776 he was promoted to a full Colonelcy. He changed the name of the house to the "Red Horse Tavern" and his son, Adam How, succeeded him in his duties as Boniface. The old hanging sign of the Red Horse is still preserved and on its back are inscribed

the names of the first three proprietors with their dates—
David How 1686, Ezekiel How 1746, Adam How 1796.

Adam's son, Lyman, closed the How record by dying a
bachelor in 1861. It was under Lyman's régime that Longfellow came to Sudbury and since his time and for all time
the tavern has been and is the Wayside Inn.

There were three hundred and two Sudbury men at Concord and Lexington led by Ezekiel How and How, himself,
was in the fight at the North Bridge.

The Red Horse was the first stop for the western mail
coach from Boston. The mail left at three A. M. and was
due at Sudbury for breakfast. It was also the stop-over for
the farmers with their market wagons traveling from the
Connecticut valley to Boston.

Washington rode past the Inn in 1775 on his way to take
command of the army besieging Boston and on his tour of
New England in 1789 stopped with landlord Ezekiel How.
Lafayette was accomodated here during his journey to Boston in 1824 and was allowed the garret over his chamber
for the use of his slaves.

Longfellow came to the Inn in its palmy days of 1840
and with Parsons, who was the poet of the "Tales," Monti,
the Sicilian, and Treadwell, the theologian, acquired the
habit of spending his summers at the Inn.

After the death of Lyman How in 1861 all the old furniture was sold by his heirs and the old house was unoccupied
until 1896 when it was reopened by Mr. and Mrs. Edward
Lemon. It has quite recently (1923) been purchased by
Mr. Henry Ford and continued as a Tavern and so furnished
from the colonial period as to make it in fact a museum of
great value to students without the confusion incident to

too great an accumulation at one spot. With rare patience Mr. Ford has sought out and found many of the original pieces and replaced them in their proper setting.

The original Inn built in 1683 is the three story gambrel facing the high road. The ell (left) was added about 1800. It is now painted yellow with white trim. It stands back a short distance from the high road in a tract of land including orchards and meadows of an area of 2,200 acres. At the right of the house is an old-fashioned formal garden with charming statues in the greenery and a bust of Longfellow at the end of the walk.

In the main portion of the building are four large rooms on the ground floor opening from a hallway of fair width running from front to rear. The ceilings are low and show the oak summers and framing. The fireplaces are not of unusual size.

To the right of the hall is the taproom, a high railed bar in one corner, with a "portcullis" which may be lowered when the bar is closed. Between the taproom and the room back of it, which was formerly used as a small social hall, is a store-room whose door is pierced with the many wounds left by the barkeeper's pick which he threw at it between drinks.

Beyond the social hall in the ell is the kitchen, well supplied with utensils of the period. Most curious is the brass device for turning the roast in the Dutch oven.

The front room to the left, that is the parlor, is now devoted largely to the memory of Longfellow. In this room, were the tales told, presumably, around the fireplace, though as a matter of history the tellers of the tales were never all together at one spot at one time. Here hang the portraits of those who were the models from which the artist drew his portraits. Ole Bull for the musician, T. W. Parsons, the translator of Dante for the poet, Luigi Monti for the Sicilian, Professor Treadwell of Harvard for the theologian, Henry Ware Wales for the student, Lyman How for the landlord and for the Spanish Jew, Isaac Esdrelin.

Next to the parlor is the bedroom in which Washington slept. To the left of this in the ell is a large room now used as restaurant and dining room.

The staircases are simple and have no turns. They lead to four large bedrooms named for their famous visitors; Lafayette, with a small room adjoining for his valet, Edison, Longfellow and Parsons. These rooms also show the framing, which is painted white, and are furnished with authentic furniture. Mr. Edison's room is always ready for him and no one else is allowed to sleep in it.

Over the restaurant in the ell is the ballroom, well proportioned, with two fireplaces, the woodwork in white. The fireplaces have as andirons bronze Hessian soldiers facing each other, the second of the two soldiers marching in the same direction away from the fire, typifying American feeling toward Hessian troops. The old box seats border the room with their hinged covers providing receptacles for the ladies' cloaks and the gentlemen's surtouts. A raised platform at the farther end is provided for the musicians.

On the third floor of the main building are seven bedrooms for the use of travelers.

Few of the old New England homesteads are as rich in their historical background as the Wayside Inn and in but few is the picture of the early day presented to the visitor with such faithfulness and such restraint.

At the outbreak of the Revolution the provincial congresses sought naturally among those who had had military training in the previous frontier wars, for officers to train and organize their raw levies. The contest with the French along the northern border had ended with the Treaty of Peace in 1763 only twelve years previous and many New England soldiers who had gained their epaulettes in that campaign were available in 1775, yet through their recent close association with the British army espoused the British side in the dispute or at least were lukewarm toward the patriots.

Among New England soldiers none was better known to both the British and his own countrymen than Colonel Israel Putnam. His family had founded Danvers in 1634 and he himself was born in Salem in 1718. Brought up on his father's farm he married and raised a family of four sons and six daughters. In 1740 he moved to Pomfret, Connecticut, and in 1755 his public life began with service in the French and Indian War. As captain of a company of volunteers from Connecticut he was sent to reduce Crown Point. In this campaign he had the aid of Massachusetts and New York troops under the command of Captain William Johnson. He distinguished himself by great bravery in the fighting about Lake George and Lake Champlain and was given his majority by Connecticut on his return in 1757. In 1759 he fought with Amherst at Ticonderoga and Crown Point and was with him at the fall of Montreal. At the close of the war he returned to his farm at Pomfret with the rank of Lieut. Colonel. He received the news of the battle of Lexington while ploughing his fields, and the story is told that he abandoned plough and oxen without further thought, mounted his horse and rode through to Cambridge, a distance of sixty-eight miles, in the same day. A regiment

The General Israel Putnam House. Danvers, Mass.

was at once organized and Putnam was given the rank of
Brigadier General. At this point the British reached him
with an offer of a sum of money and the rank of Major
General in the British army. This offer was refused. With
Prescott, he superintended fortifications of Breed's Hill
and with his own regiment stationed on Bunker Hill he
held the British in check, defending his field piece during
the encounter himself.

When Washington took command Putnam was made a
Major General and was one of the four Major Generals
authorized by Congress. After the fall of Boston he was
placed in command of New York and was present at the
battle of Long Island. After the evacuation of New York,
he was sent to Philadelphia to fortify it. In 1777 he was
in command of the Highlands above New York but was
removed on account of the loss of forts Montgomery and
Clinton. He was taken by paralysis while with the army
but lived until 1790.

Fifty-seven years of age when the war broke out, still in
the prime and vigor of his powers, he spent himself for his
country without stint. The Revolution was a testing time
which brought out the best and the worst in men and from
it Israel Putnam emerges as one of the most gallant figures
of his time.

The original John Putnam came to Salem in 1634 and
the oldest section of the Putnam homestead, to which the
General finally retired, was built in 1648. The gambrel-
roofed addition was joined to the old house in 1744. The
older part was built by Thomas, son of the emigrant and
the addition by David, oldest brother of the General. The
older is of the plain peak roof end chimney type while the

gambrel is of the central chimney tradition. The combining of the gambrel, peak and end lean-to in the one house produces a bizarre and interesting effect. The interior of the older section has many typical features though the fireplaces have been bricked up. The later section faces south and retains its shallow entry and stairs against the chimney, common to that period. The main room of the house is now on two levels with pillars marking the line at which the old joins the new. The combination forms a room of fine proportions. The house contains many relics of the General including a contemporary portrait in pastel.

The Revolutionary leaders of the first levies were not all experienced in earlier campaigns. One of Washington's most valued aids developed with the war itself, entirely without previous military training. John Glover was born in 1732 and at the outbreak of the war was an influential sailing master and fisherman of Marblehead, Massachusetts. When the news was received, he recruited a regiment of fishermen of which he was made Colonel and marched them to Cambridge. Here he rendered important service in drilling the patriot army. During the retreat from Long Island his regiment proved itself one of the most valuable of the force. It was given the difficult task of guarding the boats during the embarkation and when the army had crossed to the mainland, that of protecting its rear. It was Glover's regiment also that transported Washington's force across the Delaware during the night of Christmas 1776. His men actually rowed the boats which carried the troops. The next morning with great gallantry he led the advance in the capture of Trenton. His regiment was named the "Marine" and the "Marblehead" but Washington Irving affectionately called it "the amphibious regiment of Marblehead fishermen."

In 1777 he was made Brigadier and aided General Schuyler in the defeat of Burgoyne at Saratoga. His regiment was given the honor of transporting the captured British

The John Glover House.   Marblehead, Mass.

army to Cambridge. In 1778 he was with General Greene in New Jersey and later with General Sullivan in the Rhode Island campaign.

His house at Marblehead was built in 1762. He had loaned large sums to the Continental Congress and the end of the war found him a poor man. In one of the upper rooms of this house he undertook, when he returned, to eke out a living for his family by returning to his early trade as cobbler.

The house follows the fashion of the day along the north shore as a small gambrel three story oblong. It has two rear additions, one made in the General's time, the other by the present owner. The builder manifested classic leanings as shown by the simple doorway and by the excellent carved oak mantel, frieze and door jambs in the parlor done in the manner of McIntyre. The stairway is good but simple. In fact the note of the whole house is its simplicity, purity and harmony of line.

Patriotic sentiments were far from unanimous in New England when the break with the mother country came. In Deerfield, Dr. Williams, the town clerk, the minister, the judge, the sheriff, the esquire, three doctors, the town treasurer, one store keeper, two of the three tavern keepers and most of those who had held commissions in the French War were Tories. The Whigs were decidedly in the minority. In spite of this a town meeting was held in August, 1775, the "Sons of Liberty" organized and a regiment of Minute men recruited and sent to Cambridge. Loyalist officers were compelled to sign agreements to obey Congress and not Parliament. Major Salah Barnard was haled before the Committee of Safety accused of communicating with General Gage but was acquitted after examination, and Deerfield celebrated its declaration of Independence June 25, 1776, and erected a Liberty Pole at the end of the village street.

In a section so strongly Tory, Colonel Joseph Stebbins stands out the ardent patriot who staked his all on the fortunes of his country and risked his life and fortune to bring her liberty. His family had lived in Deerfield from

The Colonel Stebbins House. Deerfield, Mass.

the beginning. John Stebbins, son of John of Northampton, born in 1647, was in the Lothrop massacre at Bloody Brook and was the only member of the company who escaped unhurt. In the attack and massacre of 1704 he was captured and taken to Canada.

The Joseph Stebbins with whom we are concerned as early as 1774 manifested his strong Continental leanings by refusing to be married by the Tory parson of Deerfield. Instead, he drove his affianced bride, Lucy Frary, to Hinsdale, New Hampshire, where they were married by the Rev. Bunker Gay, an avowed Whig.

Stebbins had been trained with the militia train bands and held a commission as a lieutenant. At the call to arms he marched with a company to Cambridge. He was there made captain and served in Colonel Brewer's regiment at the battle of Bunker Hill. When the news came of Burgoyne's probable attack on Bennington, he marched with a company from Deerfield to that town, arriving after Stark had routed the British; he marched on to Batten Kill, joined the regiment of Colonel David Wills of Shelburne and took part in the battles of Stillwater and Bemis Heights. From the battle of Saratoga, he served through the Revolution receiving his commission as lieutenant colonel in 1781 and as colonel of the second Massachusetts Regiment in 1788.

The Stebbins mansion, built about 1772 by the father of Colonel Stebbins, is an excellent adaptation of the three and one half story, square gambrel roof house to the classic tradition. The two substantial end chimneys permit the wide central hallways on both floors and the large fireplaces in each room. The classic leanings are seen in the quoining of the corners, the cornice and the doorways, the front entrance showing particularly good work. The home stands today practically as it was during the Revolution.

The room to the left of the entrance called the South Room has a bed press built into the house with a double door which made it possible to store a double bed in it. Across the hall in the room called the "Best Room" the fireplace wall is completely paneled, the large panel over the fireplace itself measuring three feet ten inches in length and a trifle less in height. Back of the South room was the original kitchen now divided into two rooms but showing the old hearth-stone and brick oven. The two most unusual features of the house are the high cellar and the huge garret covering the entire building. The cellar is eight feet six inches high, the walls of stone and at the base of the South chimney is a huge fireplace with a brick oven, used presumably for the home manufacture of soap or some similar function required by the self supporting homestead of the time. In like manner the attic, a story and a half high, showing the chimneys and the heavy framing, but properly floored and lighted, served as a meeting place for spinning and weaving where the women of the village gathered and produced their homespun garments and incidentally exchanged the news of the day.

Colonel Joseph Stebbins had thirteen children, a worthy family for this sturdy old mansion. The house after various transfers passed to his grandson, Mr. George Sheldon, the historian of Deerfield and is now the homestead of his great granddaughter.

CHAPTER IX

THE REVOLUTION

(Continued)

WASHINGTON'S letters from Cambridge in July, 1775, show clearly the great difficulties which he encountered in the training of raw militia and in the organizing from the bottom up of all the services needed by an army. Men of such military training as Israel Putnam and John Stark were rare but the fires of patriotism were burning fiercely and fusing character out of the raw material of the English stock of New England, and so there rose out of the ruck from the shore and from the farm such gallant and able officers as John Glover and Nathaniel Greene, without previous training but with native capacity and an undying conviction of the righteousness of their cause. Washington had an instinctive understanding of these men and drawing on their full capacities he stimulated and encouraged a rapid development in them and so through the laborious months of the summer and the winter of '75 and '76 the little army of sixteen thousand men about Boston grew steadily more responsive to their commander until in March when he was confident they were ready, by a single strategic operation in the occupation of the heights of Dorchester with the cannon he had collected from near and far, the victory was won without a blow. Boston was evacuated and

Howe sailed away to Halifax with his British army and its American Tory sympathizers with whom the patriots could well dispense.

When Washington arrived in Cambridge he was first assigned to the house of the President of Harvard but that

The Vassall-Craigie-Longfellow House. Cambridge, Mass.

dwelling proving inadequate, the John Vassall home was prepared for him by the Committee of Safety.

During the period preceding the Revolution, Cambridge had become the favorite residence of rich loyalists who had built there many handsome and dignified dwellings, the gardens and lawns of which had begun to have somewhat the finished atmosphere of England itself. One of the best of these

mansions was the Vassall house, built in 1759, which became
the headquarters of the Commander in Chief. The Vassals
came originally of French stock, but the builder of this
house, John Vassall, was the grandson of Lieut. Governor
Phips who left him in 1757 a part of his ample fortune and
enabled him soon after his graduation from Harvard to
establish for his family this dignified residence. Vassall
and his wife were, however, aristocratic and strongly Tory
in their sentiments. As patriotism grew more intense the
feeling of the community against them increased in bitter-
ness until in 1774 the house was surrounded by a mob and
the lives of its inmates threatened. Taking refuge in Boston
they left with the British army when Boston was evacuated
and from Halifax sailed to England. In 1778 John Vassall
was exiled and his estate confiscated by Congress.

When it became evident that the General would be held
at Cambridge for some months, plans were made to move
his family from Mount Vernon to his headquarters. The
passage of Madam Washington across the northern states
from the Potomac, with her four horse carriage and black
postilions in red and white livery was a spectacle only
slightly less stimulating to the countryside than the transit
of her distinguished husband in the preceding summer.
The General's nephew, George Lewis, and her son, John
Park Custis, and his wife were her only companions but she
was shortly followed by Edmund Randolph as master of
ceremonies. They arrived somewhat before Christmas at
Cambridge and establishing there a miniature Republican
court, the Vassall mansion became the first official residence
in which was represented the centralized power of the
United colonies.

After the evacuation and the departure of Washington
and his family for New York the house remained vacant
for some years. In 1781 Nathaniel Tracy, rich ship master
and merchant of Newbury, bought it as one of the many
residences at which he broke the journey from Newbury
to Philadelphia. Here he gave a banquet to Admiral
d'Estaing at which he served the celebrated frog soup.
When he lost his fortune after the war, the house passed
through Mr. Thomas Russell to Dr. Andrew Craigie who
had been apothecary-general for the army during the Revolution and had amassed a fortune through various specula-
tive enterprises. His wife was Elizabeth Shaw, daughter
of the Rev. Bezaliel Shaw of Nantucket.

During the Craigie régime the house was noted for its
elaborate entertainments. Dr. Craigie built an ell on the
rear and enlarged the northeast room which he paneled
entirely in white, that it might be used as a banqueting hall.
After more than twenty years residence here Dr. Craigie
also became bankrupt and when he died, in 1819, his widow
had but little with which to maintain the mansion and was
compelled to rent suites in the house to eke out her income.
In this manner Edward Everett and his young wife lived
here as did Willard Phillips and Jared Sparks.

Longfellow came to Harvard as a professor of English
in 1837 and took rooms with Mrs. Craigie. It was a notable
group of young men which foregathered with him there,
including Lowell, Felton, Agassiz, and Charles Sumner. By
his marriage to Miss Frances Appleton of Boston in 1843
the house came to him as a gift from her father and continued its character as the center of an intellectual coterie
whose names are household words to Americans.

Longfellow was interested in maintaining the colonial tone of the house and but few changes have been made since those instituted by Dr. Craigie. When the property came to Longfellow it included eight acres of garden. Part of the land was somewhat later sold to Dr. Worcester and on it the latter built a home in which he completed his dictionary.

The entrance hall and the rooms on both floors have high paneled wainscoting and in each room one wall is completely paneled. Staircases rise from front and back halls to a common landing at which they are separated by a Palladian window and turn toward the front and rear. The parlor, at the left of the entrance, was used as Mrs. Washington's drawing room while that at the right was General Washington's office.

Harmonious in both front and side elevation, this square, substantial house is an excellent adaptation of the English classic to the American tradition. It is eminently fitting that so satisfactory an example of our best colonial architecture should have become the home of the most beloved of American poets.

Famous also in the period of the Revolution and the years following for lavish hospitality and for the ardent patriotism of its owner was the Spencer-Pierce Homestead of Newbury, Mass. Although neither the builder nor the exact date of building are definitely known, the older section was certainly in existence before 1670 and it is therefore one of the oldest of the substantial houses of New England.

The first John Spencer came over on the *Mary and John* in 1635 with Rev. Thomas Parker and others and settled on the bank of the river named Parker in later years

The Spencer-Pierce House. Newbury, Mass. South Front.

in honor of the first minister.   He was captain of a battalion
sent against the Pequot Indians but was condemned by
the General Court as a follower of Mrs. Anne Hutchinson
and the Rev. John Wheelwright for holding erroneous religious opinions, was discharged from his command and

The Spencer-Pierce House.   Newbury, Mass.   Rear View.

sent back to England.   His son remained and sold the
farm in lots.   One of these consisting of three hundred acres
was deeded to Daniel Pierce in 1651.   Pierce went to New
Jersey with others in 1665 and returned in 1670.   In all
probability he built the house we are considering before or
after this journey.   The brick and tile used in its construction were imported, since no manufacture of such
materials existed on the north shore at that date.   Such

expenditure was possible to Daniel Pierce known to be a man of wealth. He was a friend and supporter of the Rev. Thomas Parker during the protracted religious controversy which racked Newbury for a generation. Daniel Pierce, Jr., his son, was prominent in the civil and military activities of Newbury. He was honored by the first choice of pews in the Meeting House. Franklin Pierce, fourteenth President of the United States, was a descendant of this family. In 1778 the property was sold to Nathaniel Tracy, a man of great wealth for those days. Besides the stone house he had a large mansion on State Street in Newbury, a large farm at Medford, the Vassall house in Cambridge and several other residences. He boasted, in fact, that in traveling from Newbury to Philadelphia he could stop every night of the journey in his own house. A young man at the outbreak of the Revolution and an ardent patriot, he risked his fortune without hesitation in the cause of the colonies. In 1775 he fitted out the first of the privateers to prey on British commerce. The vessels so equipped were small and carried but few guns but were handled by fearless and able sailors and brought in many prizes to Boston and Newburyport. During the war he owned one hundred and ten merchant vessels which carried cargoes of great value. Most of these vessels were lost or captured and at the conclusion of peace but thirteen vessels were left to him. During this period he captured one hundred twenty-one vessels and took more than two thousand prisoners. The stores taken were those intended for the British army and his operations were of inestimable value to the cause. The captured cargoes were sold for large sums which acted as at least temporary props to the collapsing finances of the young Republic and in addition he loaned Congress out of his own resources $167,000.

While success lasted he was quite the "Grand Seigneur," his entertainments were the most elegant, his horses and coaches the finest in New England. In 1786, however, he was bankrupt. All went to his creditors except this Newbury farm which was secured to his family and here he spent the remainder of his days. His widow sold the place to Captain Boardman, ship owner and merchant. During the War of 1812 from his windows which look out across meadow land to the mouth of the river, the Captain distinguished the British ship *Friends* tacking off shore as having lost her bearings. He at once manned whale boats with men and concealed arms, rowed out to the vessel and offered to pilot her. The offer was accepted, she was boarded and piloted as a prize into the harbor of Newburyport.

The original house (right end) is a two and a half story stone building with central chimney and without lean-to. The frame addition with its separate entrance (left) was added in Captain Boardman's time, that is after 1797. The walls of the old house are two feet thick and built of granite mixed with other stone and brick, all overlaid with a thick coating of plaster. There are two windows and a niche over the main door enclosed in arched masonry, now covered with vines. The door itself is cut in two in the Dutch fashion; its upper section is protected by an inner shutter which can be raised and lowered by block and cord. The door hinges are twenty-four inches in length. Between the outer door and the original entry there is another set of doors and behind these doors the narrow stairway rises against the chimney. The rooms are about twenty feet square with deep window embrasures, some paneling and low ceilings. Summers and girths are exposed.

The west entrance (left) marks the line of the frame addition built after the Revolution. The rooms at this end are paneled in the Georgian style. The second chimney built outside the rear of the old house is used for the kitchen.

The sinews of war were painfully lacking during the entire eight years of the conflict and at no time was the army adequately equipped, uniformed or supplied. This was due not to the poverty of the people nor to the lack of natural resources. The country was not rich in the sense that England was rich, yet the people were well-to-do, there were practically no poor, they were fairly educated and were intelligent, and of raw materials there was no limit. The lack therefore was in organization. Again and again Congress accepted loans from patriotic citizens and never discovered the means to repay them. The paper currency, in which the army was paid, fell so low that ten continental dollars were exchanged for a penny. Generals had frequently to pledge their personal credit to obtain the uniforms with which to clothe their naked soldiery. Intelligent finance was therefore one of the most pressing needs of the budding Republic. Among our early financiers, Colonel Nicholas Gilman and his son, John Taylor Gilman, of New Hampshire, were distinguished both for their patriotism and the high quality of their service.

The father of Colonel Gilman was an officer in the French and Indian War of Queen Anne's reign and Nicholas served as a lieutenant under his uncle Peter in operations around Lake George in 1755. Following the fall of Quebec he served in many civil and military capacities under the Governors

Wentworth and at the beginning of the Revolution was
Colonel of the 4th Regiment of Militia and served during the
war in that capacity. On the morning after the battle of
Lexington, Nicholas' son, John Taylor Gilman, marched
with a hundred volunteers form Rockingham County and

The Ladd-Gilman House.   Exeter, N. H.   Front View.

joined his father's regiment at Cambridge where he was
made sergeant of his company and later was placed on his
father's staff and made Commissary for the three New
Hampshire regiments. Colonel Gilman's regiment was
present at the battle of Saratoga and aided in the capture of
Burgoyne's army. The important work, however, of both
father and son was done in government positions, particularly
in financial organization for their state and the united col-

onies. Colonel Gilman was chosen Treasurer and Receiver General of New Hampshire for the period from 1775 to 1783 and continental loan officer from 1777 to 1783. In these capacities he issued continental currency. He was also a member of the Committee of Safety and of the Governor's

The Ladd-Gilman House. Exeter, N. H. Rear View.

Council. In 1783 his son succeeded him in the loan office and became well known as a financier. Somewhat later he was elected State Treasurer and finally under the new constitution he was elected governor on the Federalist platform and held office from 1794 to 1805. In the latter year the Republicans came in to power and elected their candidates for the next eight years. In 1813 public sentiment swung back to the Federalist party and Gilman was re-elected

governor for three years. Though opposed to the War of
1812, he did all in his power to protect the coast of New
Hampshire during the hostilities. In 1816 he declined a re-
nomination as governor.

The Ladd-Gilman house of Exeter, N. H., became the
rendezvous of many of the political and military leaders
of the Revolutionary and post Revolutionary period including General Sullivan, General Nathaniel Folsom, Meshack
Weare, members of the Society of the Cincinnati of New
Hampshire, and Daniel Webster.

The original building (right front) was built by Nathaniel
Ladd in 1721 on part of a lot bought of Eliphalet Coffin.
The property remained in the Ladd family until purchased by
Colonel Nicholas Gilman, Sr., in 1747. It was enlarged by
the addition of the rear ell (left hand front) to accommodate
the son, Nicholas, Jr., and his bride in 1752. The original
portion is built of brick but was covered with clapboards to
correspond with the addition, the whole forming the long
low irregular succession of buildings without any particular
unity of design but with a certain dignity due to its commanding position on the side hill and the splendid elms
surrounding it. The older building was used as the state
treasurer's office during the Revolution. This accounts for
the two entrances. The house is now owned by the New
Hampshire Society of Cincinnati and contains an interesting collection of Revolutionary relics.

One of the most dramatic engagements of the Revolution
was the battle of Bennington, August 16, 1777. The first
decisive victory of American arms, the unexpected success
of the mountain boys, aided by the New Hampshire and
Massachusetts farmers, was so complete that it proved the

capacity of these untrained levies to meet the professional soldier of Europe on equal terms and encouraged the flagging spirits of the Continental leaders in the same degree that it made difficult the enforcement of the royal will.

Bennington was first chartered in 1749 by Benning Wentworth, Governor of the colony of New Hampshire, and the town was called Bennington in his honor. It was not, however, until 1761 that the actual settlement took place with the arrival of six families and their belongings. Bennington's history practically begins with the Revolution and takes its flavor from the romantic life and deeds of its frontiersman and hero, John Stark. Born in 1728, his boyhood was past amid the alarms of Indian fighting on the frontier and as a boy he was captured by Indians and held for ransom. The ransom was paid by a relative and he was restored to his family. In gratitude for his release he worked in the forest until he had accumulated logs in sufficient quantity to repay the loan. He won his epaulettes in the French and Indian War. In 1755 he was commissioned lieutenant and three years later he was with Abercrombie before Ticonderoga. He served until the conclusion of the war and came out of it with a reputation for bravery and military skill. After the battle of Lexington he was commissioned as a Colonel and recruited a battalion of eight hundred men. He marched with his men immediately to Cambridge and it was his regiment that held the right of the colonial line at Bunker Hill and repulsed three times the Welsh veterans opposed to them.

After the evacuation of Boston he was ordered to New York and was made a Brigadier by General Gates. At Trenton he was in command of the right wing. In the following spring many promotions were announced but Stark was overlooked. He was painfully disappointed by the apparent lack of appreciation of his notable services on the part of Congress and resigning his commission retired to his farm.

When Burgoyne's advance developed in the summer of '77 Stark was asked to command the New Hampshire troops. He accepted the commission with the understanding that he should act under orders from his state alone and pursuant to this agreement was sent to Bennington with an independent command.

Major General Lincoln was ordered by General Schuyler to march the New Hampshire troops to the Mohawk valley. Stark refused to move them out of the state but offered to cooperate by defending Bennington. Burgoyne was informed of this apparent insubordination and decided to take advantage of it and at the same time seize the stores known to have been collected at the Continental storehouse at Bennington. On the 15th of August, Colonel Baum reached a hill about seven miles from the village. This hill he fortified by surmounting it with breastworks of logs and mounting his guns behind them. He had in his first contingent two hundred Tories, one hundred Canadian rangers, one hundred Frazier marksmen, fifty chasseurs, three hundred and seventy Hessians and one hundred and fifty Indians, a total of nine hundred and seventy. Stark had a force of one thousand seven hundred and fifty including one thousand New Hampshire militia, five hundred Green Mountain boys and two hundred and fifty Massachusetts militia. He drew his men up in the early dawn and addressed them:

"My men, yonder are the Hessians. They were bought for seven pound ten shillings per man. Are you worth more?

Prove it. Tonight the American flag floats from yonder hill or Molly Stark sleeps a widow."

Skilled in forest warfare, the Americans took advantage of the natural cover to storm the redoubt and so neutralized the enemy's advantage in artillery. The battle became a hand to hand conflict with the result never in doubt. Baum was shortly reinforced by six hundred to seven hundred Hessians and a second obstinate engagement followed. In this second encounter the accurate fire of the colonial troops was particularly effective. Colonel Baum and Colonel Pfister in command of the Tories were both mortally wounded and two hundred and seven British and Hessians lost their lives. Stark's force took seven hundred prisoners, four cannon and a large quantity of ammunition and supplies. The Americans lost a hundred men.

This effective check to Burgoyne, including the loss of an entire regiment, added to the feint of Benedict Arnold which caused the retirement of St. Leger to Oswego and the victory of Herkimer at Oriskany made possible the capture of his entire army a month later. The battle in itself was one of the most brilliant engagements of the war.

The Eldad Dewey house in Bennington sheltered a large number of John Stark's men the night before the battle. In this house also the women of the village that same night baked loaves of bread in quantity for their consumption the following day. The kitchen where the baking was done was in the rear ell but the house was giving hospitality to so many that night that even there the women had to pick their way among the sleeping patriots as they prepared the dough for the oven.

The house was built in 1765 by Eldad Dewey the third

son of Parson Dewey and is still occupied by his descendants.
The interior has been considerably modernized but the entrance hall still boasts an excellent French wall paper antedating the Revolution. Although in its exterior the house
makes some pretension to classic decoration in its quoined

The Eldad Dewey House. Bennington, Vt.

corners, gabled cornice and its porticos, the interior maintains the simplicity of the farm homestead of the Revolution, the wall paper mentioned being its only tribute to the
fashion of the time.

In Stark and Putnam, Washington found capacity fitted
to make him general officers, ready to his hand, the product
of the bloody campaigns of the preceding French wars.

In contrast to these men, Nathanael Greene, on whose acknowledged ability and absolute loyalty the Commander in Chief came to depend perhaps more than on any other of his officers, had had no previous military experience not even, in fact, an adequate general education, and his native

The General Nathanael Greene House. East Greenwich, R. I.

capacities to meet the requirements of his high office were developed under stress of the war itself.

Born in Warwick, R. I., in 1742, Nathanael Greene was the fifth in descent from John Greene of Salisbury, England. John, the emigrant, followed Roger Williams to Massachusetts and, forced to flee as Williams was on account of his religious opinions, followed him again to Rhode Island where he founded the family. Nathanael's father was a Quaker who did not believe in education and destined him to the anvil and the plow. The son, however, was keen for education and managed through his own ingenuity and the help of friends to educate himself. The friend who was most helpful in his efforts was Dr. Stiles then a teacher and later president of Yale College. In 1770 his father made him superintendent of properties which he owned at Coventry, R. I. This gave him the opportunity to make himself known and he was chosen a member of the Rhode Island Assembly. In this body he soon demonstrated his broad viewpoint by inaugurating a plan for a school system and in 1774 he was placed on a committee to revise the militia laws of Rhode Island. Moved by the need of military training, he joined an organization known as the "Kentish Guards" as a private. Soon after he went to Boston and bought a musket and persuaded a British deserter to return with him and train the "guards." That musket is still preserved in the Greene household.

In the meantime he accumulated a library and continued his own education but his activities did not accord with the views of the Quakers of that day and both he and his brother were publicly "removed from meeting." Nevertheless his career developed along the line he had laid down for it, which shortly included matrimony, for not long after, his marriage took place to a niece of the Governor of the State.

When the news of the battle of Lexington reached him he called the "Guards" together and marched them toward Cambridge. The movement was, however, stopped by the Tory Governor whose messenger reached them as they were crossing the State line. Nevertheless Greene with two brothers and one other continued and reported to the army at Cambridge and from that time until peace was declared he continued in the military service of his country.

Rhode Island authorized an "army of observation" 1,500 strong, pending the decision as to the united action of the colonies and Greene was placed in command with the rank of Brigadier. A letter to his wife written about this time expresses his belief in the cause in which all his energies were enlisted: "Our cause is the cause of God and man. . . . I am determined to defend my rights and maintain my freedom or sell my life in the attempt and I hope the righteous God that rules the world will bless the armies of America."

After the evacuation of Boston, General Greene marched his brigade to New York via New London as part of the Continental army. In August he was commissioned Major General, one of the four authorized by Congress. In the fighting about New York, though he was ill during the battle of Long Island, he showed great bravery and unusual military capacity and following Washington's retirement to the heights above the city he was placed in command of Fort Constitution on the Palisades. Already he was rated a military genius of the first rank. At Trenton he was in command with General Sullivan and from this time on was very close to Washington and enjoyed the complete confidence of his Commander. He made the recommendation to Congress that Washington be given the supreme command and this recommendation was followed. Somewhat later he was sent to Congress as Washington's representative to counteract the underground plotting against the Commander in Chief and this mission brought additional powers to the General. With Washington he spent the winter at Valley Forge and in this time of depression when the prospects of the colonies seemed at the lowest ebb he proved himself not only a military genius and a successful politician but an organizer of exceptional ability. At Washington's request he assumed the organizing command as Quartermaster General, retaining his rank as Major General.

As the war dragged on without success in the north, British policy turned to the southern colonies where the Tory element was a strong factor and from Charleston overran South Carolina and Georgia. Greene had resigned the office of quartermaster general and as Gates was making but little headway he was given the difficult task of clearing the states involved, in his place. As his available force he found a meager twenty-three hundred men on paper with not more than fourteen hundred present, ninety cavalry and sixty artillery and of these not over eight hundred men properly uniformed. There was no food in the commissary and no money in the treasury. To obtain uniforms he was compelled to pledge his personal credit. The only favorable feature in the situation was found in his subordinate officers who were, like Francis Marion and Daniel Morgan, men of courage and ability and well versed in the conditions of the country. Against him was a well equipped British army of thirty-two hundred. Out-numbered and out-classed he could not successfully meet the enemy in the field but by superior strategy and knowledge of the country he could and did out-general him. Many of his battles, such as that of Guilford Court House, were classed tactically as defeats but strategically were victories. Cornwallis was compelled to retire to Wilmington, his nearest contact with the British fleet, and Greene turned south to Camden. His first engagement with Lord Rawdon was unsuccessful but he returned later to the attack and Rawdon was compelled to retire towards Charleston. The difficulties of supplies and re-enlistments continued until by the brilliant engagement of Eutaw Springs the British were driven into Charleston. This was on the very day, September 8, on which the joint army of Washington and Rochambeau united with that of Lafayette, finally completed the isolation of Cornwallis on the Yorktown Peninsula.

South Carolina voted the General ten thousand guineas but Georgia still remained in British control and to complete his undertaking he detached as large a force as possible with Anthony Wayne in command to recapture the State for the Continental army. After a few months campaign he was able to report to his Commander in Chief that "Georgia is ours," and the result of Wayne's successful campaign was the final evacuation of Charleston. Greene entered the city as the "Savior of the South" and was presented with a plantation by the State of Georgia. Here his wife joined him in 1782 and in 1783 at the conclusion of peace he laid down the cares and responsibilities which he had borne with such conspicuous devotion for eight years. He met Washington at Trenton where he received the personal thanks of his Commander as well as those of Congress. The joy at receiving these merited tributes was somewhat dimmed by a demand made upon him for payments covering the necessary uniforms for his southern army which threatened to sadly deplete his modest resources. His plan was to divide his time between his southern plantation and his Rhode Island home but he lived only three years after the declaration of peace and passed away in 1786 in Georgia.

The Nathanael Greene house at East Greenwich, R. I., has been so altered by modern additions that it is difficult to recognize the original section. The square main building with its single chimney, however, shown in the illustration, without the bow-window, was built by James Greene who came from Massachusetts with Roger Williams in 1685. General Greene was born in this house and it is still owned and occupied by his descendants. The interior has been changed and modernized much as has the exterior and but little to indicate its ancient origin remains. The house has been called "The Forge" from an anvil and one or two anchors found about the place.

The war of the Revolution was waged not only on the land but also on the sea and not only was British commerce seriously hampered by the numerous small craft sailing as privateers but serious losses were inflicted on ships of war and merchantmen alike by organized American naval forces such as the squadron which operated from French ports under the command of Admiral John Paul Jones. The same methods were adopted on the American coast as in European waters, that is, the organization of a squadron of the largest ships available to attack nearby British possessions in the absence of the British fleet and individual vessels of that fleet when they could be taken. Early in 1776 such a squadron was organized and equipped and Esek Hopkins of Providence, R. I., was made Commander. Hopkins was born in Scituate, R. I., in 1718 and was the brother of Hopkins, signer of the Declaration of Independence. He came to Providence before 1752. In 1775 he was appointed Commander of a battery of six eighteen pounders at Fox Point and later in charge of a battalion of six hundred to repel an invasion contemplated by the British fleet. He assisted in building a floating battery, fire ships and the laying of a chain across the channel. It was at this time that the necessity of a fleet was called to the attention of Congress and its organization authorized. Esek Hopkins was given the command with the actual rank of Admiral though he was generally called Commodore. His ships consisted of: *The Alfred*, Captain Salstonstall; *The Columbus*, Captain Whipple; *The Andrea Doria*, Captain Biddle; *The Cabot*, Captain Hopkins, the Commodore's son. Three were later added to the fleet at Philadelphia; The *Lexington* of fourteen guns, a brig under John Barry; the *Hornet*, ten guns; and the *Wasp*, eight guns.

The fleet was first sent against Lord Dunmore who was raiding the Virginia coast and put to sea February 17, 1776. In place of attacking Lord Dunmore whose force was far superior to his small ships, he attacked the British fortress at the Bermudas. The results were eminently successful. The marines which he landed captured the governor, the lieutenant governor and a member of the Council as well as one hundred cannon and large quantities of ammunition and supplies. In addition to this he captured the British schooner *Hawkes* and the brig *Bolton*. All his prizes were landed at New London in April. For this very successful enterprise the Commander received the thanks of Congress. Another attempt was against the British man of war *Glasgow* of twenty guns. This was an unequal contest and the *Glasgow* escaped. For the failure to capture her the Commodore was censured and was haled to answer charges at the bar of Congress. He was defended by John Adams and was acquitted, much to the gratification of his friends. Among those who congratulated him was his fellow sailor, Admiral John Paul Jones. Ordered to take command again he was

The Admiral Esek Hopkins House.   Providence, R. I.

somewhat dilatory in sailing and was again summoned before Congress. This time he refused to obey the summons and in 1777 he was dismissed from the service. His bravery and his loyalty to the cause were, however, never questioned. His son continued as a captain in the navy and sailed from Boston in 1779 in command of a squadron which captured British vessels and many British officers.

The Hopkins house in Providence was built in 1756 and until 1906 was occupied by the same family. The Admiral's granddaughter at that time gave the homestead to the city with four acres of ground as a park, to be preserved as a memorial. The original house is of the end chimney, two story Rhode Island type with the ell (right) as a later addition.

The Connecticut coast suffered often from the raids of the British fleet stationed at New York. The most notable of these raids was that against New London conceived and executed by Benedict Arnold after his treachery in 1781. The Shaw mansion was one of the few buildings which escaped the destruction which was then visited on the unprotected community.

The land on which the house stands was purchased in 1734 by Captain Nathaniel Shaw who lived in a frame house near by until 1755. In the latter year there arrived at New London a vessel with three hundred of the expatriated Acadians on board. As it happened, a larger number were sent here than elsewhere in Connecticut. Many of these refugees were house builders by trade and as Captain Shaw was planning to build a new home he employed them to remove the granite ledge which overlaid the hill on the side of which the house is built and to build the house itself. At the time of the Revolution the homestead was occupied by the Captain's son, Nathaniel Shaw, Jr., a man of great wealth for the period. He was absent from home on a trip to Montauk when the raid took place and much of his property was destroyed. The homestead was fired in several places by the British soldiery with the expectation that it would shortly be consumed. A Mr. Christophers,

The Shaw House. New London, Conn.

however, who lived in the adjoining house and to whom Mr. Shaw had been kind, watched the operation from his hiding place and when the soldiers had departed, crept in and put out the blaze and thus preserved the old mansion for future generations. Among many valuable articles which escaped the fire were Mr. Shaw's papers, including a letter from Benedict Arnold written from West Point, August 10, 1780, a month previous to his act of treason, in which he requests Mr. Shaw to act as his attorney for the disposition of his property in Connecticut and to transfer the funds to him at West Point. Also included were letters from Washington forming part of the correspondence between the General and Mr. Shaw.

Mrs. Shaw died here from a fever contracted through caring for the many sick and friendless prisoners landed at New London under her husband's supervision. The house was a center of much importance during the entire period of the war. Here at various times came Washington, Governor Trumbull, Lafayette, General Greene, Admiral Hopkins and Nathan Hale.

Washington visited New London in 1756 when he was only twenty-four years old and again in 1776 on his way to New York after the evacuation of Boston. At the latter visit he came on horseback in a quiet and unpretending manner, attended only by two officers and a colored servant. Commodore Hopkins had just returned from a successful raid on New Providence, Bahama Islands. Part of his fleet was in the harbor and he was landing prisoners and stores. General Greene arrived also the same night with part of his brigade and so New London celebrated the presence of the three commanders of the country's sea and land forces on the same day. Washington was the guest of Nathaniel Shaw and here he conferred with the Connecticut Committee of Safety. The chamber in which he slept, with its bed, curtains and other furniture, remains as it was when he occupied it. Lafayette was greatly moved on visiting this chamber during his stay in New London in 1824 and knelt by the bedside for some moments before leaving it.

The mansion was purchased by the New London Historical Society in 1907 and its ample chambers now house a large collection of historical relics. The first floor has two large and dignified front rooms opening from the entrance hall which bespeak a family of wealth and social importance. The hall runs through to a rear door which opens on a classic terrace facing a formal garden against the hill. The broad stairway runs from the rear hall to a landing, turning right from the landing to an equally broad hall above, hung with revolutionary portraits. The rear façade of the two stories is an excellent example of the English classic design. The house is constructed of stone from chimney to foundation.

Another source of loss to the planters of the Connecticut shore as well as an aid and comfort to the British army in New York, was the illicit trade with the enemy carried on by Tories living among the colonists. This trade was directed from Long Island and by 1781 assumed such proportions that the town of Guilford voted to "detect, suppress and stop" it, "esteeming our greatest danger to arise from that quarter." The special charge of enforcing the provisions of this resolution fell on Captain Samuel Lee who was Commander of the coast guard at that point. To suppress any part of this traffic required that the Captain with his coast guard should be constantly on the alert to detect and seize the malefactors as well as their supplies and this kept him cruising the Sound and away from his home a large part of the time. Contraband articles were brought to the house and stored in the cellar. The protection of these supplies was left to his wife, Agnes Dickinson Lee, a woman of unusual courage and resource.

The captain left a cannon as a protection and when, during his absence the Tories raided his place in the attempt to recover their contraband, as often happened, Mrs. Lee fired the cannon to alarm the neighborhood who ran to her defense; and when neighbors were lacking she had to depend on her nimble wits which seldom failed her in an emergency.

The result of this vigorous enforcement of the law, was the development of an intense hatred for the Lee family on the part of the Tory element. The townspeople even more than the Lees were constantly in fear of retaliation which took the shape of burning barns and other buildings and many threats against their lives. With her alarm gun Mrs. Lee was the first to arouse the countryside at the landing of the British at Lett's Island in 1781.

Captain Lee himself was a remarkable product of the times. Fearless and devoted to the cause of the patriots he was at the same time a typical Puritan of the rigid New Haven school, a debater of biblical subjects and doctrinal questions and given to writing his opinions on controversial questions. Of the most conservative element in New England himself, his house expresses his mental attitude. Although it was built in 1763 it partakes, as do so many of the Guilford homes, of the characteristics of the Massachusetts houses of the early XVIIIth century. With its single chimney, short front roof, heavy cornice and long lean-to, it might have been built at any time after 1675. This is the kind of house in fact that Washington found to be still typical when he revisited Connecticut in 1789.

The counsels of wisdom were fortunately not wanting to direct the political activities of the colonists during the

The Captain Samuel Lee House.   Guilford, Conn.

progress of the war and to establish the new state on a firm foundation when peace was concluded. Although during the early years of the conflict Congress as a body was woefully lacking in the energy, courage and resource which were characteristic of the Commander in Chief, as the conflict dragged on the States sent their younger men to Philadelphia, many of them the product of the Revolutionary period and of the new conceptions of the time so rich on both sides of the Atlantic in liberal doctrines which were before long to lead to the freeing of the Third Estate in France and the Bourgeois Revolution throughout Europe. Among the leaders of this group of young men Oliver Ellsworth of Connecticut came to be one of the most brilliant.

Born at Windsor, Connecticut, in 1745, his ancestor, Josiah Ellsworth, was an emigrant from Yorkshire in 1650. He entered Yale and followed the course for two years but finished his college training at Princeton where he was granted the degree of Master of Arts in 1766. Thereafter he pursued the study of law until he was admitted to the bar five years later. During and after this time, however, he was compelled to devote no little attention to a lumber business in which he engaged to earn enough to pay for his education. After he was admitted he took the lease of a farm for three years and during this time walked to and from Hartford, ten miles each way every day, as he could not afford a horse. His receipts from the law at this time did not average more than three pounds per annum. Before long however his clients began to increase and in a few years he attained to a large practice and was made the Attorney General of the State. He was then considered the leader of the Connecticut bar and Noah Webster, who was a student in his office, has said that his docket averaged from one thousand to fifteen hundred cases. In 1775, at the beginning of hostilities, when he was thirty years old, he was elected a member of the Connecticut Assembly, and in 1777 he was sent to Congress and remained a representative of his state for six years. For four years he was a member of the Governor's Council and from 1784 to 1789 Judge of the Supreme Court of Connecticut. In 1787 he was a member of the Council which framed the Federal constitution and to him with Roger Sherman and Paterson of New Jersey is due the fact that we have a Federal rather than a Centralized National Government. He was one of the first senators from Connecticut and was chairman of the Senate Committee which organized the country's Judiciary. Called the "Firmest pillar of Washington's administration in the Senate," he came to be of great influence, was elected Senator a second time and in 1796 was appointed Chief Justice of the United States. Three years later he was sent to France on a special mission with William R. Davis and William Vans Murray. Honorary degrees were conferred upon him by Yale, Dartmouth and Princeton, and in 1807 full of honors and in the ripe maturity of his powers he died at Windsor.

The land on which the Chief Justice's house, named "Elmwood," is built, was bought by Josiah Ellsworth in 1665 and remained the property of the Ellsworth family until it was deeded in 1903 by one hundred and sixteen heirs, to the Connecticut Society of the Daughters of the American Revolution. The square main portion of the house was built by David Ellsworth in 1740 and thirteen elms about it were set out by his son Oliver, each named for one of the original states. The colonnaded portico addition was made by the Chief Justice to give the house an air of greater elegance according to the ideas of the time. Here he entertained many of the leaders, including Washington and Adams. Among many interesting pieces of the period the house contains a Gobelin tapestry which was the gift of Napoleon, and French wall paper prized for its suggestion of European culture.

The Oliver Ellsworth House.   Windsor, Conn.

In his diary under date of October 21, 1789, Washington writes: "By promise I was to have breakfasted at Mr. Ellsworth's at Windsor on my way to Springfield but the morning proving very wet and the rain not ceasing until past ten o'clock, I did not set out till half after that hour; I called however on Mr. Ellsworth and stay'd there near an hour." [1]

That the figures, the faces and the costumes of the men who shaped our destinies in this critical period of our history are familiar to us, as well as the portraits of their contemporaries in England, is due, in large part, to the prolific execution of the American contemporary painter, Gilbert Stuart.

Born in Narragansett, R. I., in 1755, he was named Charles Stuart, his father being an ardent Jacobite, but he exchanged Charles for Gilbert when he became of age. As a boy he painted portraits and when only fifteen years of age was taken to Europe by Cosmo Alexander, a Scotchman, who kept him abroad for two years. When his patron died he was compelled to return to Rhode Island for lack of funds and set himself up as a portrait painter at Newport. Conscious of his lack of technique, his strong desire was to return to Europe for further study and particularly to work with his countryman, Benjamin West. In the spring of 1775 the opportunity came and fearing that he might not have another on account of the immanent hostilities, he went to London and persuaded West to accept him as a pupil. During the several years in which he lived with Mr. West his knowledge of music was of great value in furnishing

[1] "Diaries of George Washington," edited by Jos. A. Hoskins, Summerfield, N. C., 1921.

him the necessary income to support himself. The charm
of his personality as well as his talents made him many
friends and soon began to bring him sitters, and before he
left London he was classed as a fashionable portrait painter.

Birthplace of Gilbert Stuart. North Kingston, R. I.

In 1786 he married Miss Charlotte Coates and within
two years thereafter had painted the portrait of the Duke
of Rutland and others of the aristocracy in Dublin. His
reputation now assured, he returned to New York in 1792,
where he painted John Jay and other celebrities. Mr. Jay
gave him a letter to Washington at Philadelphia and the
interview which resulted brought him the opportunity he
had for many years desired—a sitting from the President.

Several portraits of Washington followed, that one which is named the "Atheneum Portrait" being the best known. It is said, however, that the first portrait painted was the best likeness. In 1803 he moved to Washington and two years later to Boston where he remained until his death in 1828.

Afflicted with the artistic lack of business sense he was given to reckless expenditure and left his family destitute in spite of the fact that he painted over seven hundred portraits, many being of the most famous persons of his day.

A master in the rendering of flesh, his portraits form the lifelike and vivid pageant of the Revolution for all posterity.

Stuart was famous for the geniality and charm of his conversation. His pungent expression and ready wit of themselves brought him many sitters.

The curious old gambrel roof house shown in the illustration with the mill adjoining remind us of his humble beginnings and that his career for the prolific product of which all Americans must do him homage was entirely the result of his own conscious genius and the untiring perseverance which expressed it.

The Webb Mansion of Wethersfield is the symbol of the culmination of the Revolutionary drama so far as New England is concerned, since in its front parlor, now called the "Council Chamber," was held that conference between Washington and the Comte de Rochambeau which brought about the co-operation of Rochambeau's force, the fleet and Washington's army at Yorktown, the capitulation of Lord Cornwallis and the end of the eight years struggle.

Joseph Webb, the fourth of his name and the builder of this house, was descended from Richard Webb who migrated

from Cambridge to Connecticut with Hooker in 1636 and
lived variously at Stratford, Norwalk and Stamford. His
grandchildren returned to the Connecticut Valley and
settled at Wethersfield and here in 1752 Josiah Webb built
the house fronting the main street and during part or all

The Webb House. Wethersfield, Conn.

of the time he lived in it, ran it as a Tavern. Joseph however
died in 1761 and his widow married Silas Deane who had
been associated with Benjamin Franklin in negotiating the
French treaty and was a man of prominence in the Connecticut Valley. His house was next door and the family retained both houses, the Webb mansion becoming the residence of Mrs. Dean's son, Joseph Webb, and his young bride.

Wethersfield was at the Revolutionary epoch a rich and prosperous town. Washington had stopped here earlier in the war and had visited Silas Deane and other well known citizens. At the date mentioned he desired a conference with Rochambeau at a point not too easily discovered to arrange the details of the movement the outcome of which was so completely satisfactory to the colonies and their allies. Samuel Blatchley Webb, younger brother of Joseph, a Colonel on Washington's staff is credited with the suggestion of the family homestead as meeting the conditions desired by the commander in chief.

To this council Washington invited the Comte de Rochambeau, the Comte de Barras, the Chevalier de Chastellux, General Knox, General Duportail, Governor Trumbull and Colonel Wadsworth. The council lasted five days. The French officers and their suites were entertained at the Deanes and at other homesteads while Washington made his headquarters at the Webb house. A Sunday intervening, Washington was asked at what hour he preferred divine service. He replied that he desired no change in the usual custom and at the usual hour he would be present with his officers. The entire council with its aides were present therefore at the opening hymn and we may be sure were the cynosure of all eyes.

This rectangular gambrel roof end chimney house represents the transition from the single chimney, narrow entry type since, in spite of its central hallway and stair, it retained the summer beams which are the characteristics of the old order. The pilastered portico, windows and doorway express the classical leaning of the period. There is good paneling in the rooms on both floors. The rear ell is an older construction than the main building and originally stood where the main building now stands and was moved back and turned at right angles to it when the latter was built.

The coup which resulted from this council was brilliant in conception and carried out with extraordinary energy and secrecy. Although the original plan contemplated a joint attack on New York, and this was what was expected by General Clinton, the operations of Admiral Grasse in the West Indies which indicated his rendezvous at the mouth of the Chesapeake in August, determined Washington in favor of the bold plan of transferring the bulk of his army four hundred miles to the south where Lafayette was already holding the neck of the peninsula. Rochambeau marched his four thousand men across Connecticut in July and made the juncture with Washington and on August 19 the combined armies crossed the Hudson at King's Ferry. By September 5 they had reached the head of Chesapeake Bay and on September 26, Washington arrived before Yorktown. It was not until the army was marching through the streets of Philadelphia that General Clinton became aware of its real objective and then it was too late. A six weeks' siege with but little fighting brought the capitulation and the end of the war.

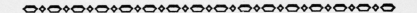

CHAPTER X

HOMES OF PROSPERITY AND CULTURE

T HE change in the thought of the communities which made up the territory of New England from that of a people owing fealty to a power across the seas to one which carried its own responsibility for government and welfare did not at once translate itself into living conditions nor was it at once made manifest in the building of its dwelling houses. The change which was working and at first inclined Americans to seek their architectural models from the French rather than from the English, finally determined a greater independence of contemporary European design and turned the budding architects of the new Republic to original classic sources and produced a renaissance of its own which in its use of Greek and Roman models antedated a similar adaptation in Europe. Although the prophet of this new doctrine was Thomas Jefferson and its first and most notable development in Virginia, the northern states with equal enthusiasm reacted to its influence.

The awakening, however, did not come about with equal rapidity in all parts of New England. The more conservative sections clung to their conservatism, the more progressive and those at the seaboard more closely in touch with the world consciousness substituted more quickly the new for the old.

Education was from the beginning a responsibility of the state to the individual, recognized in the Puritan settlements as second only in importance to religion. Beginning with the child it carried him through childhood to adolescence and when he had acquired the reasoning power it offered him, if he were capable of assimilating it, the philosophy of the ancients adapted to the Puritanical point of view, in the early centers of learning, at Harvard, Yale, Princeton and Dartmouth. With the change in political thought, education and religion walked hand in hand, and as a need of lawgivers, physicians and engineers developed from the expanding community life, these professions in greater degree became the product of the higher institutions in place of their restriction to the field of religious training.

Education, therefore, was one of the connecting links between the old and the new, between the colonies and the Republic, varying its rate of progress with the community which each institution expressed, yet steadily, though at differing pace, marching onward toward the universal, liberal, and largely material education of our day.

The early days discovered and developed teachers of no mean ability in the field of secondary education. Ezekiel Cheever was the head of a grammar school which prepared students for Harvard as early as 1650 and had Cotton Mather as one of his pupils. Joshua Coffin, following the Revolution, a master beloved of his students, is known to us also through his most eminent pupil, the poet Whittier.

In 1762, Samuel Moody was master of a grammar school at York, Maine. His ancestor was one of the first who settled along the Parker River and from that beginning until his time the family was known throughout the Puritan colonies for their piety, their patriotism and occasionally for their eccentricity.

Master Moody graduated at Harvard in 1746 and as master of the York Grammar School became known throughout the colony as a teacher of unusual qualities. From this important task he was invited to assume one of greater influence as the head of the Dummer School at South Byfield, Mass., which was at that time and for many years after the only school whose avowed object was the preparation of students for a collegiate course. This school, the plant of which at the time he took charge consisted only of the Dummer Mansion and one school house, he conducted in its every detail for nineteen years. Much of this time the Mansion House alone housed more than a score of the pupils, while the total enrollment, even with the school's meager facilities, reached seventy or eighty. Among its students were several who rose to eminence as officers of the Revolutionary army and Navy, in Congress and in the councils of the first President, not to forget two future Presidents of Harvard College and Samuel Phillips, through whose efforts were founded Phillips Exeter and Phillips Andover academies.

The Dummer Mansion, so far as is shown by the available evidence, was built at some time between 1716 and 1720 by William Dummer who, during this time was lieutenant governor of Massachusetts Bay and it was used presumably as his summer residence. In 1714 he married Katherine Dudley, daughter of Joseph Dudley, former lieutenant governor of Massachusetts Bay. Her portrait and that of her sire hang still in the Dummer Mansion. Samuel Shute succeeded Dudley as Governor and William Dummer, his son-in-law, was made lieutenant governor. When Colonel Shute, exasperated beyond the bounds of his patience by the opposition of the General Court, returned to England in 1723 Dummer became the acting Governor and for five years continuously and also in the interval between the death of Governor Burnet and Governor Belcher was the chief magis-

The Dummer Mansion. South Byfield, Mass.

trate of the colony. This office he administered apparently with greater tact and more satisfaction to the colony than his predecessor or those who succeeded him.

He was much interested in education and, by his will, his dwelling house, this mansion, and the farm on which it was built were devised to trustees to be administered for all time as a grammar school, the income to be used for the erection of a school house and to support a master. Governor Dummer died in 1761, the school house was erected the year following and the school opened under Master Moody in 1763. From that time to the present day this school, which was incorporated later as the Dummer Academy, has trained and sent forth its students in increasing numbers to every walk of life and has continued to carry out the will of its founder in so doing. It is now the oldest unendowed school in the country.

The mansion, two and one half stories, with dormer windows, has one gable with two chimneys and one gable with only one. It shared with the Warner house of Portsmouth in being one of the most elegant mansions of the period. The end walls are of stone divided by bands to mark the lines of the two stories, while the front and rear walls are of frame. The design of the house permits the central hallway and stairs with the chambers opening from it on both floors and has made easy and natural the transition to the Georgian decorations of doors, windows and cornice which followed. The ell built of stone with its own chimney provides the kitchen and servants quarters. The hallway is paneled throughout and there is good paneling in the drawing and reception rooms. The broad stairway with low risers lends plausibility to the traditional story that on the day he brought his bride to his mansion, William Dummer rode his horse up these stairs to the second floor.

The traditional conservatism of Connecticut is in no phase of its development more noticeable than in the building of its later colonial houses. At the period when its contemporaries in Massachusetts were designing the square Georgian mansions of classic ornamentation, Connecticut was merely translating frame into brick as an indication of wealth and importance without changing the design or the detail of the older building. This is notably the case with the Robbins house of Rocky Hill, Connecticut, built in 1767.

The Robbins House. Rocky Hill, Conn.

Rocky Hill, for most of its history a part of Wethersfield and known as Stepney Landing, was in the years preceding and during the Revolution a prosperous community of great activity in ship building. From this port on the Connecticut River sailed many ships to Cuba, Porto Rico and other ports in the West Indies until in the first quarter of the XIXth century the trade of the river towns was transferred to the seaports with better facilities for handling larger craft.

The Robbins family was one of the oldest of Stepney parish, the name appearing frequently in the early records. This house was built by John Robbins, Esquire, the wealthiest and most influential of his family and of this community, in 1767. During the Revolution the house was used as a Tavern. The hanging signboard, marked 1773, with a figure on horseback said to represent the Duke of Cambridge, is still in the possession of the family. This old sign is perforated by bullet holes; not an evidence of war, as Stepney Landing was never the scene of battle, but probably the result of a jollification or some early celebration of the Fourth of July.

The house is built of the first native brick produced in Connecticut and set on foundations of dressed stone from which rise two and one half stories capped with gambrel roof and dormer windows. A circular window in each gable is added for decoration, above the attic windows, and there are three main chimneys and a rear kitchen ell. The floors are marked in brick by transverse lines crossing the end walls. While, in its absence of decoration this house is as simple and plain in detail as can be imagined, its lines are good. It stood in its day as the expression of prosperous and comfortable living and was considered one of the finest mansions in the colony. The substantial character of its construction makes it now one of the best preserved mansions of the period in New England. Until 1914 it remained the home of Robbins descendants.

In the more progressive communities a transition period took place between pre-Revolutionary and post-Revolutionary building, between the traditional early house, whether gable or gambrel roofed, and the square brick house with classic decoration. The form which this transition took

varied in different communities. In Nantucket the Macy
house represents the connecting link between the simpler
central chimney frame gable with lean-to, such as the Captain Joshua Coffin house and the post-Revolutionary brick
houses with classic decoration. In this house the end chimneys

The Macy House. Nantucket.

are substituted for the central chimney; and the fence, the
entrance porch and the doorway become important features.
The Captain's walk, so strong a leaning of Nantucket houses,
remains, and the height of the old houses, two stories and
an attic, is also preserved. The actual date of building is not
known but was probably not long before the Revolution.
It possesses a beautiful mahogany stairway with treads, balusters and fluted spindles of the same wood. This house has

always been and is now occupied by Macys. The original Macys were among the first settlers and later generations were owners of whaling craft during the golden period.

From the frame Georgian house with end chimneys it is but a step to the more definite acceptance of the classic in the later brick houses, and next to the Macy house on Main Street stand the three brick mansions, exactly alike, built by Joseph Starbuck for his three sons, George, Matthew and William, in 1837. The Starbuck family is one of the oldest in Nantucket and like most Nantucket families has intermarried with the Coffins and other clans descended from the original settlers.

Joseph, in early life a butcher, became a whaling merchant and as such was unusually successful. He had five children, three boys and two girls. For the three sons he himself provided homes, as mentioned, and the sons-in-law, Nathaniel Barney and William Hadwin, both built handsome houses themselves, the home of the latter at the corner of Main and Pleasant Streets boasting the high-pillared portico of the American classic type then coming into vogue.

In the George Starbuck house, as in other Nantucket Georgian houses, the gable roof is visible, and the belvedere and the balustrade are important features. With these decorative additions as well as the Ionic portico, window pediments and the elaborate iron fence, we have the complete acceptance of the Georgian tradition, the classical finish on dwellings whose construction follows the old design. The warm red brick of these and other mansions of Main Street add much to the warmth of color and the atmosphere of hospitality breathed by that delightful old street.

The George Starbuck House. Nantucket.

The Jared Coffin house of Nantucket, known as "Moor's End," is another somewhat larger specimen of the same period and type. This house retains the traditional Nantucket front steps with a classic portico in the jog, while the plain entrance door has a fan light to enliven the regularity of the façade.

The Jared Coffin House.   Nantucket.

While in the south, during the early years of the Republic, the tendency of building among the slave-holding aristocracy was toward the classic in outline as well as in decoration, in the north the influence of the merchant prevailed and this influence is expressed in the square three story, hip roof mansion of frame and later of brick with classic decorations. In these houses the frame house represents the transition between the old order and the more elaborate brick mansions which followed.

The Cook-Oliver house on Federal Street, in Salem, was built from plans by Samuel McIntire between 1804 and 1815. Much of the interior woodwork as well as the fence was

The Cook-Oliver House. Salem, Mass.

originally hand carved by McIntire for the Elias Hasket-Derby house and was transferred to this house when the latter dwelling was torn down. This house was built for Captain Samuel Cook, master mariner, the construction progressing only as fast as the profits of Captain Cook's voyages permitted. Its completion, therefore, was delayed eleven years. The use made of the finish from the older dwelling has fortunately preserved much of McIntire's best work.

Up to 1885 this was the residence of General Henry Kemble Oliver, Captain Cook's son-in-law, who, during his career was Mayor of Lawrence, Mass., treasurer of cotton mills, State Treasurer, Adjutant General of Massachusetts and finally Mayor of Salem when he was eighty years old. Incidentally a musician and a composer, he was the author of the well-known hymn "Federal Street," and other compositions.

In this house we have the typical square, three-story mansion of the period in northern Massachusetts, with a two story ell and jut-out. The walls are covered with clapboards except on the east side where the wall is of brick. The window lintels, the simple harmonious portico, the band across the front connecting the portico and the house, the heavy cornice, the gate posts surmounted with their classic urns are all details in which McIntire excelled. The façade is relieved by the foreshortening of the third floor windows as was customary at that time.

The Pickman-Shreve-Little house of 27 Chestnut Street, Salem, built in 1816, is one of the best examples of McIntire's design and execution as applied to brick construction. The design has not changed materially from the frame house which preceded it and the difference between the two is found principally in the greater richness of detail. The portico is Corinthian instead of Ionic or Doric and the fence and railing of wrought iron in place of wood, while the Palladian window is used to relieve the severity of the façade as well as to lighten the hall of the second floor, while the fan light performs a like function for the third floor.

The Pickman-Shreve-Little House. Salem, Mass.

The cornices are heavier with added ornamentation, as are the window pediments with their decorations in stone. The portico is quoted as the best hand carved wood Corinthian portico in the country.

Though rich in detail the house is not overloaded but is unusually harmonious in effect. Among the many dignified patrician mansions of Chestnut Street this is one of the most satisfying.

In the academic shades of Cambridge many of the old Tory mansions remain, similar in type to the Craigie-Longfellow house described in Chapter IX. One of the most interesting architecturally as well as for its associations is "Elmwood," the birthplace and home of James Russell Lowell. Known in earlier days as the Mansion House it was bought from Elbridge Gerry by Lowell's father, the Rev. Charles Lowell, pastor of the West Street Congregational Church of Boston, in 1818, and James Russell was born here in 1819. He married Maria White, sister of a classmate, and brought his bride to Elmwood. Here he wrote the "Biglow Papers" and many of his other works and to the old homestead he returned after many years absence as our representative in Spain and in England, in 1889. In November of this year he writes to Mrs. Leslie Stephen: [1]

"It is a very strange feeling, this of renewing my life here. I feel somehow as if Charon had ferried me the wrong way, and yet it is into a world of ghosts that he has brought me, and I am slowly making myself at home among them. . . .

"But Oh! the changes! I hardly knew the old road (a street now) that I have paced so many years, for the new

[1] Letters of Jas. Russell Lowell, edited by Chas. Eliot Norton, Harper & Bros., 1894.

The James Russell Lowell House. Cambridge, Mass.

houses. My old homestead seems to have a puzzled look in its eyes as it looks down (a trifle superciliously methinks) on these upstarts. . . .

"It is odd to think that the little feet which make the old staircases and passages querulous at their broken slumbers are the second generation since my own. I try to believe it but I find it hard. I feel so anomalously young I can't persuade myself that I ever made such a rumpus, though perhaps the boots are thicker now.

"The two old English elms in front of the house haven't changed. The sturdy islanders! A trifle thicker in the waist perhaps as is the wont of prosperous elders but looking just as I first saw them seventy years ago, and it is a balm to my eyes. I am by no means sure that it is wise to love the accustomed and familiar so much as I do but it is pleasant and gives a unity to life which trying can't accomplish."

In the following January he pictures to the Misses Lawrence in England the old mansion and its surroundings as he then sees them. He calls it "a pleasant old house twice as old as I am." This would make the date of its building 1748. He speaks of Cambridge as "now a populous suburb," and continues with his description of the house:

"It still has some ten acres of open about it, and some fine old trees. . . . It is a square house with four rooms on a floor, like some houses of the Georgian era I have seen in English provincial towns, only they are of brick and this is of wood. But it is solid with its heavy oaken beams, the spaces between which in the four outer walls are filled in with brick, though you musn't fancy a brick and timber house, for outwardly it is sheathed with wood. Inside there is much wainscot (of deal) painted white in the fashion of the time when it was built. It is very sunny, the sun rising so as to shine (at an acute angle to be sure) through the northern windows, and going round the other three sides in the course of the day. There is a pretty staircase with the quaint old twisted banisters, which they call balusters now, but mine are banisters. My library occupies two rooms opening into each other by arches at the sides of the ample chimneys. The trees I look out on are the earliest things I remember. There you have me in my new-old quarters. But you must not fancy a large house—rooms sixteen feet square and, on the ground floor, nine high. It was large, as things went here when it was built, and has a certain air of amplitude about it as from some inward sense of dignity."

Still more elaborate than Elmwood is the pre-Revolutionary frame mansion built by Joseph Nightingale of Providence, in 1769, best known by the name of its later owner, John Carter Brown. In this house we still have the square three story hip roof but with much greater elaboration of ornament. In the double deck of the roof the walk is preserved, as this was a ship owner's mansion, built on the side hill with an excellent view of the harbor. The quoined corners, the handsome balustrade with its urns, the heavy window pediments and the free use of classic orders made this one of the elegant mansions of the golden period of that aristocracy of merchant princes which followed the Revolution.

John Carter Brown, the second owner of the mansion, born ten years after the Revolution and graduated from Brown University in the class of 1816, inherited an ample

estate and was by means of it enabled to satisfy his scholarly
tastes in the acquisition of rare and curious books.   His
first purchase was Sewall's "Apocaliptica."   Following this,
with much study, rare patience and a large expenditure of
time and money, he collected from all parts of the world

The John Carter Brown House.   Providence, R. I.

the largest and probably the best collection of books on
American history in existence.   Many of the volumes are
the contributions to the subject by foreign authors, ranging
from the letters of Columbus of 1493 to the political pam-
phlets of 1800.   The catalog includes among original sources
more than six thousand letters by contemporary writers,
of inestimable value to historians.

This library was at first stored in this mansion but was later moved to the fire-proof Grecian temple on the Campus of Brown University, a gift also of Mr. Brown. He became trustee and a fellow of the University and after his father, was its greatest benefactor. His wife was Sophia Augusta

The Edward Carrington House. Providence, R. I.

Browne, daughter of Patrick Browne, Governor of the British Island of North Providence and descended on her mother's side from Roger Williams.

The Edward Carrington house, another of the patrician mansions of Providence, stands on William Street around the corner from the John Carter Brown house and at about an equal distance from the John Brown Mansion described in a previous chapter. These three houses express admirably, that he who runs may read, the wealth, the culture, the refinement of taste and the high architectural standards of the aristocracy which passed away, along with its taste for good building, after the first quarter of the nineteenth century.

This society whose foundation was commerce was enriched by contact with the University in its midst, whose needs it was privileged to supply, and on its side the University was greatly enlarged in its scope in so standing side by side with the world of affairs.

The Carrington house, built of brick after the Revolution, retains the square bulk and hip roof of the earlier houses but is distinguished by its elaborate double portico. In this feature, as in the line of the rear ell suggesting slave quarters, it has something of the flavor of the manors of Virginia and Maryland. The colonial tradition is maintained in the doorways, the gate posts with their urns and many other features.

Mr. Edward Carrington was United States Consul at Canton and a prominent and successful China merchant and brought many works of art from the Orient which still adorn the mansion. He was prominent as a banker and influential in building Blackstone Canal, which was completed from Providence to Worcester, but lost its usefulness after the development of the railroads.

The change in men's thoughts wrought by the Revolution, to which we have already referred, began to be expressed in a breaking away from the old traditions in their building and though a new tradition was generally accepted as the substitute for the old, in some cases, the change was marked

by a complete break and the use of a style dictated by the
purely individual taste of the builder. This was the case
at Indian Hill Farm, West Newbury, Mass., whose owner
indulged his fancy for English Manor houses without refer-

Indian Hill Farm. West Newbury, Mass.

ence to the Georgian tradition behind him or to the cult
for the classic then in vogue.

The house stands on land which was the last Indian
reservation of the neighborhood and derives its name from
this fact. The Sachem, "Old Tom," deeded it to the town
of Newbury in 1650. For many years the property was
retained by the town but in 1709 it was sold to Samuel
Poore who built a house upon it. This house was destroyed

by lightning but another was built in its place and Samuel
Poore continued to reside in it until his death in 1769. His
son, Benjamin, inherited the property and in 1832 with his
son, Benjamin Perley Poore, then a lad, visited England
and Scotland. Attracted by the English village architecture,
he decided to rebuild the old house, the third on this site,
and added the front porch and wings with dormer windows,
balconies and leaded glass, such as he had seen in England.
He provided also a lodge-gate at one end of the rambling
mansion and ample barns for his livestock and produce at
the other. To complete the picture, the entrance court has
a parterre of lawn as its foreground and the driveway is
carried to a circular terrace flanked by privet hedges behind
which on the side hill lies a formal garden divided by walks
lined with perennials and separated by more high hedges
in quite the English fashion.

Benjamin Poore was drawn to California by the gold
craze of 1849 and later to Hong Kong and was lost at sea on
his return voyage. His son, Benjamin Perley Poore, as an
attaché of the American legation in Brussels, was authorized
by Congress to negotiate with the French government for
various documents in their possession pertaining to the
American Revolution and as a result of his efforts brought
to this country ten volumes of valuable data. He later became a newspaper correspondent at Washington and clerk
of two important Senate Committees. During the Civil War
he served as Major and Lieutenant Colonel under General
Benjamin F. Butler, and after the war published a "Life of
General Burnside" and other works.

The estate remains the property of the Poore family
but the house is now only occasionally opened to show

interested visitors its varied collection of objects of historic
and artisic value from all parts of the world.

Although the Renaissance of the classic in outline as well
as in decoration drew its immediate inspiration from Virginia, New England reacted to it generally, though at varying periods and, roughly speaking, from 1820 to 1850 con-
formed its style of both public buildings and dwellings to
this model. So completely, in fact, was the country at large
taken by this cult that no building of any pretensions
whether for residence or public use was built in any other
manner. Many causes conspired to produce and foster this
sentiment. In the establishment of the Republic our forefathers used as models the Republics of Greece and Rome
and elaborated this conception of democracy with the French
philosophy of the end of the century. The leaders of post-
Revolutionary thought drew constantly upon classic sources
as a background and out of the Revolution itself came the
Society of the Cincinnati, purely Roman in its inspiration.
The War of 1812 turned Americans again more strongly
against everything English and toward French culture with
its expression in the costumes and furnishings of the Empire.
Finally the Greek War of Independence in 1821 drew heavily
on American sympathies.

The models used for both public buildings and dwellings
were first the Grecian temple, often the Parthenon itself,
in all its purity, and the Roman Rotonda sometimes with,
and sometimes without, the dome, and where neither could
be adopted in its completeness, pillars at least were indis-
pensable. In fact, during this time there was a very mania
for pillars. The cult was deep seated and practically universal and it required some thirty years for its votaries to

discover that a type of building well enough suited to public buildings, requiring lofty chambers of large area was generally quite unsuited to the needs of daily living.

This period produced architects of ability and book architecture was less used than in pre-Revolutionary building.

The William R. Rodman House. New Bedford, Mass.

Brick, if used, was covered with stucco or painted gray, while in districts such as New Bedford, where stone was abundant, this material became the universal building medium.   Among architects of the period, Russell Warren of Providence has left many notable specimens of the temple adaptation in Providence; and in New Bedford he is responsible for the present Public Library formerly the Custom

House and several other stone buildings similar in inspiration. The William R. Rodman house on County St., New Bedford, is believed to have been built by Warren. It is at any rate decidedly in his style. The date of this house is given as 1833. It passed to a Mr. Grinnell who added the third story and in 1856 was bought by Mr. Abraham H. Howland, the first mayor of New Bedford.

This mansion was one of the most expensive and pretentious of southern Massachusetts when built. Constructed of native stone, its fine Corinthian portico, solid square bulk and general severity of line conform to the classic rigidity of the design, dignified but ponderous, suggesting rather the institution than the home.

Somewhat more homelike is the Sigourney house of Hartford in which the rotonda is the main inspiration. This house was built in 1820 by Charles Sigourney. Educated at Hampstead, England, he returned to Hartford at the close of the century and established a business in hardware. He was a man of literary and artistic tastes and a strong upholder of the Church of England. As such he became a prominent member of Christ Church and was influential in the establishment of Trinity College. He married Lydia Huntley as his second wife in 1819. She had taught a select class of young ladies in Hartford and later was one of the founders of a school in Philadelphia which was the first in the country to provide a medical education for women. Before her marriage she published a volume entitled "Moral Pieces in Prose and Verse." After her marriage she devoted her leisure to literature and became one of the best known of American writers. Her ability became in later years of substantial value to her family, as her husband lost a large part of his fortune. In her "Letters of Life," published posthumously, she enumerates the product of her pen as forty-six volumes and more than two thousand articles. She was much read not only in this country but also in England and on the continent. As an evidence of her popu-

The Sigourney House. Hartford, Conn.

larity abroad she received a diamond bracelet from the Queen of the French.

While her poetry was not of the highest order, it expressed emotions of the heart melodiously, was religious in its inspiration and of universal appeal. Her prose followed the classic style of Addison and Steele. Not only was she a writer but also a philanthropist who had many pensioners, and was often known to deny herself luxuries to help the needy. Highly esteemed in Hartford where she lived for fifty years, she was favorably known also throughout the country and it is said that in this house she received a visit from every President of the United States during her lifetime except Washington and Polk. To crown her fame, her epitaph was written by John Greenleaf Whittier.

The house of brick, three stories with a wing, was the special study of Charles Sigourney in its building. He is said to have drawn the model for every detail. It contained many modern innovations, including a special summer kitchen, cooler than the winter kitchen, a laundry and a dairy. It also contained a chamber for such wayfaring man as might need a lodging for the night.

The classic model is followed not only in the rotonda but in the extension of the Ionic order to the side portico, the cornices and in other details. The mansion is now owned by the city of Hartford and is used as a school.

A more faithful expression of the temple ideal is found in the James Hillhouse Mansion of New Haven called "Sachem's Wood."

James Hillhouse was descended from an Irish clergyman of the same name who came to New Hampshire with the Presbyterian emigrants in 1719. Born in 1754, he graduated from Yale in the class of 1773, served in the Revolution and was captain of the Governor's foot guards when New Haven was raided by General Tryon with British troops from New York. He was representative in the Legislature from 1780 to 1789, member of the Governor's Council, elected on the Federalist ticket to Congress in 1796, he was later elected Senator to take the place of Oliver Ellsworth when the latter

was made Chief Justice. Re-elected in 1797, 1803 and 1809
he became President of the Senate pro-tempore when Jefferson retired to assume the Presidency.   Thereafter he was
Treasurer of his Alma Mater for several years and received
from her the degree of LL. D.

His son, James Abram, born in 1789, was a graduate of the
class of 1808 Yale College.   In business first in New York,

"Sachem's Wood." New Haven, Conn.

after a few years he retired to this estate and devoted himself to literary work.   In 1830 he built this house and here
his father died two years later.   The name, "Sachem's
Wood," followed the popular title of "Sachem," given to
the father from his marked Indian physiognomy.   The
younger Hillhouse wrote many poems, of which the one
named "Sachem's Wood" is best known.   The house, of
two stories, square, of brown stone, understood to be the

work of Ithiel Town and Alexander Jackson Davis, is an excellent specimen of the Grecian and from its commanding location still dominates the beautiful avenue which bears the family name.

History is not alone written in the annals of political development, military achievement and economic change but also in the daily life of the people as exemplifying their inheritance and the application of their traditions to problems as they arise. Religion plays an important part in this expression of their convictions and particularly is this the case with the people whose dwellings we have described. In the three hundred years since the landing at Plymouth, religious thought in New England has run the gamut from rigid theocracy to ultra-liberalism and this evolution, working through a people with whom religion has always been fundamental, is now transferred from a locality to the nation at large. This virile conviction which has come to demand a reasonable justification for its faith, however varied be its expression in the later generations, is the most hopeful leaven on which to depend for the leavening of the entire nation.

In those centers in which European emigrations of the past thirty-five years have collected in the largest numbers, its influence is felt least and correspondingly in those in which New England migrations are in the majority its influence is strongest. The outcome of liberalized religious conviction is ethical culture, and the result of a general acceptance of ethical culture is to develop a life of constructive thought with an interest in education and the arts and a desire for fundamentally clean living.

This is what we have to offer the emigrants of other races who come to make their home with us, and so long as we keep those qualities of culture and freedom of religious thought dominant will we be able to give them a concept in value beyond price. When, however, this heritage becomes diluted by differing concepts of ethics and culture drawn from different sources, our country will become a different place, whether for good or ill time alone will show.

These houses which we have described are the expression of the daily life of this people along the road of their progress during the past three centuries. Their preservation and study will help us, who are so largely a product of their efforts, to better understand ourselves.